WHEN OUR
LEADERS
do

*Help Other People in Your
Chosen Field and Discover
a Fortune for Yourself*

bad
THINGS

Mangal Dan
Dipty Ph.D.

T0145599

WHEN OUR LEADERS do **bad** THINGS
Help Other People in Your Chosen Field and Discover a Fortune for Yourself

Mangal Dan Dipty Ph.D.

ISBN 978-1-61448-144-7 Paperback
ISBN 978-1-61448-145-4 eBook
Library of Congress Control Number: 2011939626

Published by:
Morgan James Publishing
The Entrepreneurial Publisher
5 Penn Plaza, 23rd Floor
New York City, New York 10001
(212) 655-5470 Office
(516) 908-4496 Fax
www.MorganJamesPublishing.com

Cover Design by:
Rachel Lopez
rachel@r2cdesign.com

Interior Design by:
Bonnie Bushman
bbushman@bresnan.net

In an effort to support local communities, raise awareness and funds, Morgan James Publishing donates a percent of all book sales for the life of each book to Habitat for Humanity Peninsula and Greater Williamsburg.
Get involved today, visit
www.HelpHabitatForHumanity.org.

**"Help other people in your chosen field
And discover a fortune for yourself"
— Dr. Dipty**

Meet Dr. Dipty in Las Vegas or online
and receive FREE training or continuing education
at: **www.YourDecisionPlusAction.com**

ACKNOWLEDGMENTS

I wish to thank all of my clients who participated in the group discussions that are part of the domestic violence prevention program. I am grateful for the ways in which their contributions about life's most difficult questions provided valuable insights.

Thanks to the Orange County Probation Department and the Community Resources Unit for the referrals and approval of the program.

Thanks to my wife, Wendy, for her love, understanding, and patience while I was busy writing this book.

Thanks to my daughters, Evangeline, Irene, Christina, and Roseline, for reading and reviewing the chapters.

Thanks to my parents for raising me and teaching me how to read and write.

Special thanks to Spencer W. Kimball for being my teacher and mentor.

Thanks to my editors, Yvette M. Petruzelli, Karen Lynn, Dorothy Peterson, Alisz M. Demecs, and David Sequeira, for their work on this book. Thanks to Pamela Guerrieri of Proofed to Perfection for editing the entire book.

Thanks to Morgan James Publishing and staff for their talents and professionalism in producing this book.

Table of Contents

INTRODUCTION

When Our Leaders Do Bad Things is an innovative 30,000-word book that addresses the common failures those in prominence succumb to, and explains how to avoid such pitfalls evident in the media today.

There are three psychological power tools presented in this book:

1. The Three-dimensional Thinking: a decision-making tool.
2. The biological stress defense mechanism: a tool for taking action immediately. Understanding and applying these first two tools can help individuals choose the best course of action in the midst of emotional confusion—a common plight among leaders and those who live in the limelight.
3. The Negative Thinking: a precious tool to control passion, addiction, and other emotions such as greed and lust.

Many of these tools sound unbelievable, especially "negative thinking" because we have been taught that negative thinking is bad and we must get rid of it. Most people are unaware of the usefulness of negative thinking.

In addition, this book provides information about styles of communication and ways to enhance one's communication skills.

We are born here with the purpose and mission to help other people and create a better world. The world is dynamic and in constant change, which needs constant new leaders in our chosen field. It seems like the Creator of the Universe has designed a way where other people's well-being is our well-being. If we help others as leaders in our chosen field, the Universe showers us with money, wealth, fame, and prestige.

Our leaders, priests, and celebrities are role models of our society. We look up to them for answers and solutions for our problems. We admire them, trust them, and show pride in their accomplishments. It is as if we crown them with haloes—and then when we see one of our ideal people make a mistake or fall short, we feel betrayed. In our shock and surprise, we label his or her wrongdoings as "bad."

In our democratic society, we elect or select our leaders, professionals, and money managers with the hope that they will make good decisions. Their poor judgment might cost us our lives or our life savings. Their unwise decisions might cause us enormous physical or mental suffering.

Many people don't have a realistic view of leaders. We tend to see our national leaders as Santa Claus because of their generosity with tax dollars when they are giving help to foreign nations, or as Scrooge because of their stinginess to when we want them to help their own people—the ones who elected them.

The Creator has given human beings free will, as well as a built-in super power generator—our intelligence. But we must learn how to start and stop the motor and how to control the motor while it is in motion. The power and force we generate could be compared to holding an electric power saw going at high speed. We might have the intention of creating beautiful furniture, but if we do not know how to control the saw, we might make a mistake and destroy the building material instead and hurt ourselves.

Unbridled passion or force—despite our positive intention to do good—may bring negative results or even cause disasters. If we do not know—or if we forget—how to control the force generated by our super power generator, we may do bad things.

Our leaders are criticized for making decisions that provide quick fixes to bandage national problems instead of finding solutions to remove the root causes. They are also accused of using positive forces with good intentions to bring peace and justice, but instead causing mass destruction of millions of innocent people including the elderly and children.

This book—written to bring more awareness about the significant human weaknesses of ignorance, forgetfulness, and sleepiness to young students and professionals who desire to be our future leaders, priests, and celebrities—aims to help them be aware and prepared, so they can avoid mistakes that might cost them their jobs, businesses, relationships, and marriages, as well as recognition, fame, and prestige. The book also was written to help laypersons who are interested in acquiring wisdom and knowledge about the skills they will need for achievement and success. The reader will discover ways to approach everyday situations and life challenges from a positive and objective standpoint.

When people are in the midst of emotional confusion, they often focus only on the negative aspects of a situation, making it difficult for them to view things from an objective perspective. Such a viewpoint would help them explore various sources of the problems and discover positive and effective solutions.

This clarity of mind can be achieved by using three-dimensional thinking, which helps people temporarily detach themselves from situations and clearly view the positive, negative, and neutral factors involved. Doing this allows people to find the most logical and effective course of decision plus action to solve their problems.

I wrote this book to show the reader how to use this newly discovered system of three-dimensional thinking to increase their ability to make better decisions and choose better strategies to take action and easily resolve the conflicts that are blocking their moments of joy. This information includes tools and strategies for overcoming anger and stress as well as for resolving other problems.

While most of the book focuses on anger and conflicts, there is also material on how to use three-dimensional thinking for other issues such as decision-making, finding peace, establishing good communication, and overcoming addictions.

Understanding Our Perceptions and Behaviors

Chapter One uses examples of three-dimensional thinking to describe the inner workings of our thoughts, feelings, and behavior in a concise and understandable format. It explains how we label people's behavior, especially that of leaders, priests, and celebrities as good or bad. It teaches what we can do to improve our perception and why we must understand our rights and take responsibilities for our potentially negative behavior.

Three-Dimensional Thinking

Chapter Two explains our three-dimensional positive, negative, and neutral behavior. It explains why leaders, priests, and public figures may do bad things. Every individual seeks a fulfilling, problem-free life. But that's not realistic. What is realistic, however, is learning how to overcome the conflicts we face in our everyday life.

This chapter defines the concept of thinking on three levels—positive, negative, and neutral—and demonstrates how to discipline our minds in a way that we can control our feelings, actions, and reactions. This chapter focuses on helping the reader recognize and control their own thoughts, feelings and behaviors to reach their desired goals.

Skills and Strategies

Chapter Three presents skills and strategies for solving personal as well as interpersonal problems and guides the reader step by step through ways to restore communication and loving relationships.

This chapter is broken into sections that address several types of strategies and skills that can be applied by actively using our minds in everyday circumstances.

We all know what excessive stress can do to our physical and mental energy. What can we do to manage our stress levels and simultaneously increase our energy? There are many resources available—such as yoga, meditation, relaxation techniques, and sauna baths— that may help us release our physical and mental tensions. These activities are very good for our health. However, if we recognize the root cause of our stress, we can get rid of stress in seconds. The stress defense mechanism also referred to as "fight, flight, or freeze," can be used to remove the stress at the very moment an unpleasant experience occurs.

Anger is an emotion that we all experience, and it has destroyed more lives than any other emotional expression. An entire section of this book is dedicated to managing anger. This section dissects the causes and results of anger and reveals the steps we subconsciously take as anger escalates into such things as violence, verbal abuse, and self harm. By recognizing anger and its counterparts, we can more easily prevent its negative effect on us and those around us.

This practical teaching method includes self-exploratory questions as well as communication tips for dealing with bosses, supervisors, and co-workers in personal and interpersonal relationships. It also explains how habits and addictions are formed, how to eliminate them, and how to apply our minds in overcoming problems and crises.

Understanding Domestic Violence

Chapter Four reveals the causes and ramifications of domestic violence. Most people think that domestic violence occurs among illiterates or mentally ill people. It may surprise you that domestically abusive are often individuals we trust in prominent positions—executives, national leaders, religious leaders, medical doctors, business managers, business owners, educators, professional athletes, celebrities, and movie stars. Every year, reports of domestic violence increase. Even so, we can take personal measures to put a stop to violence. Chapter Four explains the types of violence that exist and shows the origins and common trigger points for violent activity. This chapter also outlines practical steps to take to end violence in our lives.

When Our Leaders Do Bad Things explores not only how beliefs and habits are essential in the pursuit of success and happiness but also how erroneous beliefs and counterproductive habits hold us back from reaching our goals. It guides the reader through using three-dimensional thinking to form positive, productive habits in place of their negative ones. The reader will learn that dualism teaches us to examine our problems or issues with only a pro-and-con approach; whereas using three-dimensional thinking examines the positive, negative, and neutral dimensions of each problem.

Throughout this book, the reader will learn to focus on the neutral dimension to find relief from negative emotions such as anger, frustration, lust, greed, fear, and disappointment. The reader also will learn to use the modified biological stress defense mechanisms for survival as well as protection from negative emotions. The reader will recognize how negative thinking and beliefs can create anger, stress, anxiety, and depression. But also, the same "negative thinking" and "negative beliefs" can help control passion addiction, greed and lust. Three-dimensional thinking has been very helpful to the clients of the Glenoaks Counseling Center for controlling anger, reducing stress, eliminating bad habits, and improving relationships—all of which decreased the incidents of domestic violence. By applying the information addressed in this program, a person who experiences anger can more easily recognize, analyze, and ultimately change his or her behavior.

As a group psychotherapist for more than fifteen years, I have provided services to more than one thousand clients who have benefited from this program. The topics and chapters in this book were written to be discussed in group sessions. Each chapter concludes with suggestions, skills, and strategies that allow the reader to make his or her own choices. Many of these ideas and concepts are repeated throughout this book, because sometimes we need to be exposed to an idea several times before we can change a counterproductive behavior.

When Our Leaders Do Bad Things is a priceless tool based on an ancient idea called "dualism," a concept created by many great thinkers, philosophers, religious leaders, scientists, and psychologists over the ages. I accidentally discovered the existence of a neutral dimension in dualism and focused on this dimension to create a new paradigm: "three-dimensional thinking."

This book teaches that positive, negative, and neutral elements exist together just as electrons, protons, and neutrons do in the atom. The positive and negative elements attract and repel. The book explains that "good" or "evil" may not accurately capture what someone is.

The knowledge in this book can provide the tools that will enhance your life and the lives of your friends and relatives. If you have wondered how you can improve your mental health or simply grow as an individual, the material presented in this book will take your hand and lead you toward a more successful life.

To the Reader

Dear Reader,

I am a student of psychology, theology, and philosophy. I was born in the small village of Murthahandi in the Eastern Ghats Mountain Range of India. I spent my early childhood in that village where there was no school for children. My parents moved to a small town called Kotapad when I was about eight years old. My parents enrolled me in a public school where Hindu, Muslim, and Christian children studied together. I enjoyed attending school because of my friends. My favorite subject was geography. I learned about Native American Indians as well as America's high-rises, irrigation systems, and Tundra forests. I thought that someday that I would visit these places. I failed eighth grade and was ashamed to repeat the same grade, so I left the school. After leaving school, I learned how to sew and sell clothes. I enjoyed selling garments at the bazaar and making money but was not satisfied with my life. I wanted to get more education, so I went to the city of Koraput. Here I attended a public boarding high school. At eighteen, I graduated, joined a theological seminary, and became a guru (teacher) of the Evangelical Lutheran Church in Kotapad. I enjoyed preaching the gospel of Jesus Christ in the villages and towns; I felt compassion for poor and sick people. My desire for learning was not satisfied. I went to Doon Bible College in Dehradun for further theological study and became an ordained minister of a small church.

In my private time I prepared to take the matriculation examination to apply to Punjab University. Once I passed the examination I then studied for the intermediate college examination, which I passed. I was then able to take courses at Agra University. I graduated with a Bachelor of Arts Degree. In 1969, I had an opportunity to come to the United States, where I attended Brigham Young University and earned a Bachelor of Science Degree. I wanted to make my living by helping others. After my graduation, I went to University of Utah, obtained a Masters in Social Work. After years of serving people as a social worker, I took and passed the State License Exam. While I was employed, I continued taking post graduate home study courses through California Coast University, where I earned Ph.D. in clinical psychology.

I had opportunities to serve people as a personal, family, and group therapist. I have served as a director of a mental health clinic in Riverside County, California. I have also served as an oral commissioner of the Board of Behavioral Science Examiners in Southern California. I had a private practice in Anaheim, California, for over fifteen years.

My education and experience with clients helped me formulate the principles behind three-dimensional thinking and biological stress defense mechanisms. To fully benefit from these tools in *When Our Leaders Do Bad Things*, I suggest that the exercises be done a minimum of three months to one year. (See Section Three of Chapter Three for more information.) Simply understanding the concept and technique is of little value without firsthand experience. You need to practice at work, at home, on the highway, at the grocery store, the banks—wherever people, things, or events seem to rob you of peace, and happiness.

Congratulations! You have made a good decision to read this book.

Best regards—

Mangal Dan Dipty, Ph.D.

CHAPTER ONE

UNDERSTANDING OUR PERCEPTIONS AND BEHAVIORS

As we discuss three-dimensional thinking, it is important to understand the inner workings of our perceptions and behaviors. This brings us to the vital questions: Why do we behave the way we do? Why do our leaders do bad things? Many have tried to answer these questions, and the truth is that there are myriads of variables that determine our and other's behavior.

Some theorists debate whether behavior, thinking, or feeling occurs first. One theory suggests that we see, think, and interpret, and then we feel and behave or act. For example, we see ice cream and think about how it would be nice to have some, and then we buy and consume it. Another theory suggests that we feel, think, interpret, and then we behave. For instance, when we feel cold, we think about how to relieve the discomfort, and then we put on warm clothes. Yet another theory suggests that we behave or do things first and then we feel, think, and interpret. For example, we impulsively light a cigarette, and then, while enjoying the sensation of smoking, we think about the implications of our behavior.

It is possible that we create our feelings by our thinking, but we also sometimes create our thinking by our feelings. And we

11

sometimes we create both feelings and thinking by our behavior. All of these theories may be correct in different circumstances.

All events, situations, and objects—including people—have positive, negative, and neutral dimensions in various proportions. We tend to focus on one dimension at a time, but the other aspects are always present.

A magician makes magic by misdirecting our perception. In a stage play or Broadway production, the audience sees only the part of the stage where the light is focused; they don't see the activities beyond the spotlight. Likewise, we see only one dimension of an object, an event, a person, or a situation where we have focused our minds and fail to notice the other two dimensions, which remain in the dark. As a result, we sometimes make mistakes by making judgments and decisions based on incomplete information.

We see the world with the lens of our memories and interpret the events and objects as they make sense to us. Our memories consist of stored images, thoughts, and beliefs from our pasts. In our memories, we have impressions of our early childhood experiences and family experiences as well as our culture, traditions, societal norms, values, and religious beliefs. We also store our knowledge, as well as our professional and personal experiences.

One example of this stored memory is if a policeman with flashing red lights stops us and gives us a citation for a traffic violation. The next time we see a policeman with flashing red lights, we will immediately think of getting another citation—even if this time the policeman is stopping someone else or on his way to another emergency. Why? Because we have stored the image of flashing red lights and the meaning of getting a citation is linked in our memories.

Individuals, groups, and societies may differ in the ways they perceive the same object, behavior, or situation. Each person filters such perceptions according to his or her own knowledge, experiences and values. We have seen these variations of perception during judicial court trials. A common phenomenon at the witness stand involves a variety of witnesses reporting vastly different observations of the same incident; each observer is convinced his/her observation was correct.

We also find extremely different perceptions among nations. The behavior of George Washington, our nation's founding father, was perceived by the British as criminal; they labeled him a traitor. But Washington's behavior was perceived and labeled by Americans as heroic. Those nations who were neither concerned about the British rule nor about American freedom. George Washington's behavior was perceived as an incident or an event. The bombings of Hiroshima and Nagasaki in World War II were perceived by Americans and their allies as a victory the greatest good and by Japanese and their allies as a defeat the worst evil. Those nations who were not involved in the World War II bombings of Hiroshima and Nagasaki felt it was an event, neither good nor evil.

There are many religions found in the world to provide the human need of spirituality. Religions can be compared with world's various ethnic foods that have properties to sustain human life. All religions claim to be correct and true. However, we must remember that each believer's statement of each religion is true to him or her according to his or her perception.

In our society, we have categorized people into two divisions: laypeople and professionals/experts. Professionals are considered the people who are leaders, priests, celebrities, executives, engineers, mechanics, lawyers, doctors, electricians, plumbers, geologists, physicists, chemists, teachers, actors, counselors, and many others who are competent in their chosen fields. A person may be a professional in his or her field and a layperson in other fields; for example, a violinist may be considered an expert in music, but still will seek the services of a professional mechanic to repair her car. Each professional sees and interprets one aspect of the world through his or her expertise with more detail and accuracy than a layperson, but his perceptions about another part of life might be rudimentary.

A medical doctor sees a human body and interprets health problems more accurately than a layperson. A geologist or a jeweler sees a rock and assesses its real value more correctly than a layperson. A chemist sees chemicals and predicts their reactions more distinctly than a layperson. Why can these professionals observe and interpret things more precisely than the layperson? It is because they have a more highly powered memory lens, which has been upgraded by their education, training, and experience.

Now we understand that what we learned from our environment (including people) creates our subconscious mind, which subconscious influences our conscious mind in making decisions and taking action. This is why it is necessary for every one of us to enhance the power of our subconscious mind by continuing our educations, so that we can improve our perception and analytical abilities and gain the wisdom to interpret the world more accurately. Reading, receiving consultation, mentoring, and counseling also can enable us to see and interpret the world more accurately.

Our feelings are generated by many sources, but mainly by outside sources, including what we eat and drink, the air that we breathe, and the environment in which we live. Feelings also are generated by our thoughts. The same factors responsible for our feelings also determine our physical and mental health.

FOOD: The food and drugs that we take into our bodies affect our feelings. Our emotional reactions can be positive, negative, or neutral, depending on the kinds and amounts of food and drugs we ingest. When we eat spoiled food or take an overdose of drugs, our thoughts become ineffective; in such cases, food or drugs can take over our bodies and minds entirely.

AIR: The air we breathe may generate positive, negative, or neutral feelings. If there is enough oxygen, we feel good. If there is not enough oxygen, we feel sleepy or dizzy. Perfume and the scents of flowers may make us feel good. When we breathe air mixed with fumes or poisonous gas, we may feel distressed or even sick. Inhaling excessive carbon monoxide makes our thoughts ineffective and may result in death.

ENVIRONMENT: The environment may influence our feelings and generate thoughts that are positive, negative, or neutral. For example, imagine that you are walking down the aisle of a grocery store and your foot slips on a banana peel. You fall down and hurt your ankle. First, you feel the hurt and pain. Then you may think, "What a stupid person I am, walking and not watching where I am going." Or you may think, "What a careless store manager who neglected to keep the store clean. I am going to sue the store manager for the compensation of my injury and pain." Or you may think, "That surprised me, but I am okay" and get up and continue shopping.

If people or circumstances physically inflict pain upon us, we will experience pain regardless of what we think. However, we may control or minimize our pain by thinking neutral or positive thoughts instead of negative thoughts.

THOUGHTS: Our thoughts also create our feelings. We feel positive, negative, or neutral according to our thinking. We behave the way it makes sense to us at any given moment, time, or situation. Generally, we don't do "crazy" things intentionally. Even if we do crazy things, it's because they make perfect sense to us at that time. How "crazy" any behavior is depends on the person viewing and judging it. It is other people who observe and label our behavior as positive, negative, or neutral.

For example, if we see a person crying, we don't know why he or she is crying. Only the person crying knows the reason why. We see the crying behavior through our subconscious mind and interpret it in a way that makes sense to us. Then we label it as positive, negative, or neutral, and respond to it accordingly.

If we interpret the person crying positively, we feel compassion and we reach out to help. If we interpret the crying negatively, we feel irritated and may shout at him or her to stop crying. If we interpret his or her crying in a neutral manner, we may feel unconcerned and walk away from the scene.

Why do leaders, priests, celebrities, and many other good people do bad things? Nobody can know that answer except them. Who labels their behavior good or bad? You and I may interpret their behavior according to our own perception as positive, negative, or neutral. Then we label that behavior as criminal, immoral, unethical, or just a simple mistake. Who labels our own behavior good or bad? The people in the world are also happy to evaluate and label our behavior, including our society and our neighbors; they assign labels according to their own perceptions.

.It is important to know and understand our rights and responsibilities in the society in which we live. Living in a city, we find laws, ordinances, challenges, competition, conflicts, and opposition as well as support, opportunities, and resources to meet our needs and wants.

We are interdependent on each other for our growth and survival. Almost anything we want or need—money, love, recognition, fame, or prestige—comes from other people. Therefore, we must learn to relate harmoniously with friends, family members, neighbors, co-workers, boss, customers, society, and our nation as well as with the world.

We make money by working, selling products, or providing services to others. Others make money by working, selling products, and providing services to us. The farmer depends on food stores to sell his crops to make his livelihood. The food stores depend on us to buy their groceries to make a living. We depend on grocery stores for our food supply.

Plants live by consuming water, air, sunlight, and minerals found in the soil. Some animals live by eating the grass and vegetation, while others live by consuming other smaller animals. Scavengers live by eating dead animals. A big fish eats a small fish. Larger animals successfully hunt the smaller ones; a predator in one situation may become prey in another. The lions, cougars, and tigers can make us their prey, but, given our insulation from the wild, we are generally safe from them. However, we are still prey to viruses, bacteria, cancer, mites, and that feed on us. We don't have a guarantee of a trouble-free life.

We do not live in the Stone Age, and most of us no longer make our homes in a wilderness or jungle where the fittest survive. Only by living alone on an island can we avoid the need to obey societal laws.

In our advanced, sophisticated, and democratic society, public welfare is a priority. We are free people, and we advocate human rights to the whole world. We want everyone to have the right to get an education, worship, choose professions, and elect or be elected to serve in the government. In this system, an individual exercises his rights to live happily but does not have the right to violate other people's rights. Individuals must learn to find happiness without taking away the happiness of others.

In this society, a person must know his rights and responsibilities. A baby in the crib is happy when his stomach is full and his clothes are dry and warm. He starts crying when he is hungry or his diaper is wet. The parents change the diaper and give him food. He plays with his toys until he gets bored, and then he cries and has a temper tantrum until he finds or is shown something else to entertain him.

Similarly, an adult gets upset and angry when his or her needs, wants, and expectations are not met. An adult may become furious or enraged and demand or force other people to meet his or her needs and wants. But in doing so, he or she violates another person's rights. This society does not tolerate the violation of human rights; it penalizes the violators to bring justice to the people.

Our society itself includes positive, negative, and neutral dimensions. The positive dimension encompasses resources, enormous strength, amazing beauty, charity, and abundance of food. The negative dimension includes hatred, prejudice, and terrible violence. The neutral dimension is vague; many people exist without a purpose in life.

We have a desire to belong, be respected, live free of fear, work with dignity, and find happiness in our lives. Our personal happiness is linked with the happiness of our partners and children. Therefore, we must be aware of our positive, negative, and neutral dimensions and those of others as we interdependently establish our rights and responsibilities with cooperation and respect for the law.

Summary

We see the world with the lens of our subconscious minds and interpret the events, objects, and persons as they make sense to us. Our subconscious mind advises our conscious mind in decision-making and taking action. We behave the way it makes sense to us in that particular situation. Other people may think that we are crazy, evil, stupid, or insane but we think that we are always right. The world, our society, community, neighbors, and friends judge our behavior. Our success, wealth, and happiness are linked to that of others. We need cooperation, love, and respect for one another to experience joy, peace and happiness and create a heavenly human society on earth.

Questions

1. Why do we behave the way we do?
2. Who labels our behavior right or wrong?
3. Why do we have to cooperate and respect others?

CHAPTER TWO

THREE-DIMENSIONAL THINKING

"The most beautiful thing we can experience is the mysterious. It is the source of all true art and science." — Albert Einstein

What an amazing time we are living in on Earth! Some proclaim that it is the best time in their lives; some say that it is the same, mundane old thing; and still others cry out that it is the worst time in their lives. Who is right and who is wrong? They all seem to be right according to their own perception and experience.

Our leaders, priests, and celebrities are having their own individual experiences of life at this time. Although we look up to them and admire them, some of them are experiencing life as pleasure; some are bored; and others are in the midst of despair. Despite the range of their experience, we feel shocked when people living public lives exhibit frustration and anger, or when they make poor choices with serious consequences.

Why do leaders, priests, and celebrities do bad things? Well, we may ask ourselves the same question. Why do law abiding, intelligent good people do bad things? It is probably true that most good people do bad things at some time in their life. This is because we are humans and not divine. Humans do make mistakes.

A mistake can be a small action that causes only minor damage. Other mistakes, however, are more serious and have irreversible negative consequences. Ordinary people and famous people alike make both kinds of mistakes.

Life is full of unpredictable challenges; we never know what we have to face the next second, minute, hour, and day. We might be tempted to do something wrong, not pay attention to the twists in the road and as result drive into a ditch, or misjudge the character of a business partner and suffer financially. We may be faced with choosing the right path at a crossroads, and we might have to make that decision in the midst of confusion, frustration, anger, or fear. We might have to deal with our own greed and lust.

Sometimes we forget or overlook the moral, ethical, or legal signposts we encounter along our life journey and as a result commit unethical acts. Philosophers Plato and Socrates believed that humans are inherently good. They believed the Creator did not design humans with of bad or evil **characteristics.** However, some humans appear to be flawed; some are born without the full potential ability to learn. They are labeled by our society as mentally retarded or disabled.

Even those of us with the ability to learn have flaws. We are born with some weaknesses such as ignorance, forgetfulness, distractibility, and sleepiness. However, our weaknesses are an important part of personal strength. We learn to read, write, and educate ourselves as well as control our forgetfulness and sleepiness through self-discipline, along with the help of reminders from other people and devices such as alarm clocks.

We are here on this planet to grow, develop, learn, and utilize good discernment and judgment so that we can live our lives successfully. We need reliable and effective tools to help us make good decisions. We need to improve our discernment and judgment in choosing the right thought, right decision, and right action in each situation, so we can be successful even in the midst of our emotional confusion. We must remember that our decisions and actions can bring success, peace, and happiness. Decision without action remains only a wish. Action without a right decision can bring disaster.

We often find ourselves in challenging situations in which we suffer economically, psychologically, and emotionally. These situations may be due to our own actions. For example, we know that we must pay our credit card bills on time, but many of us fail to do so and end up having to pay late charges. We also know that we must abide by the posted speed limits when we drive, but we sometimes chose not to heed them and end up causing accidents or receiving speeding tickets.

In other cases, challenging situations are caused by circumstances beyond our control. We may wash our cars on a bright, sunny day, but suddenly it starts raining, and we end up having to wash our cars again. You and your boss have been getting along very well, but he suddenly becomes very critical of you. Or you date someone for two years, fall in love, and decide to get married—but after the honeymoon, your partner begin to talk about getting a divorce because something went wrong during the honeymoon.

These scenarios illustrate an important truth about the world and its residents; the everyday situations we find ourselves in are dynamic and constantly changing. At times, it can be very difficult to decide how to respond to the situations that life presents. In this book, I offer three psychological power tools you can use to help deal with these unpredictable challenges. One is the three-dimensional thinking and the other is the modified biological stress defense mechanism. The third one is the Negative Thinking. Most people are unaware of the usefulness of the "negative thinking" to control passion, addiction, greed, lust and counterproductive behavior.

By applying three-dimensional thinking, we can evaluate the positive, negative, and neutral aspects of any situation to make better decisions and take appropriate action by using the modified biological defense mechanisms to improve that situation. (Modified biological defense mechanism is presented in Section One of Chapter Three.) Using this approach helps reduce suffering and improve the quality of our lives.

When we first hear the words "three-dimensional thinking," some thoughts may come to mind, like deep thinking or well-rounded thinking. But true three-dimensional thinking far surpasses that simple definition. Three-dimensional thinking isn't just intense brainpower; it is when your thoughts possess the power to change your life.

So what exactly is three-dimensional thinking? It allows people to temporarily detach themselves from challenging situations and explore the three dimensions—positive, negative, and neutral—of those situations. This exploration allows people to discover ideal solutions to their problems.

Dualism teaches us to evaluate problems by using pros and cons. For example, a college student sees a brand new car and desires to purchase it with his limited source of income. He uses the pros and cons evaluation method, which can leave him feeling frustrated. He says to himself, "If I buy the car, I might not be able to make my monthly payments. If I don't buy the car, I might get in trouble being late to my class. I don't know what to do!"

The student experiences emotional confusion because he can't decide whether or not to buy the car. He does not see the third option, which is neutral. This choice could also be labeled "undecided." By remaining undecided, he has time to think. Furthermore, once he learns of the existence of third option, he will feel relief from the emotional pressure of making an immediate decision.

The student may then begin to explore the situation by asking himself, "Do I really need the car at this time? Can I solve the problem of attending my class on time by other means, such as getting a ride or taking a bus?" By using the three-dimensional thinking method, he gives himself the choice of taking more time to consider the possibilities. Then he'll be able to make better decision about purchasing a car.

The neutral choice helps us calm our emotional arousal and provides us a window of opportunity to escape when we feel that we are stuck in unwanted situations.

Three-dimensional thinking, which can be defined as thinking positive, negative, and neutral simultaneously, can be easily learned, remembered, and practiced. It's a useful method of evaluating situations and making sound choices before taking action.

The concept of three-dimensional thinking springs from the ancient universal doctrine of dualism, which frames things as good and evil, positive and negative, trust versus mistrust, honesty versus dishonesty, and selfishness versus altruism. Dualism focuses on opposite sides, polarities, or dichotomies. We can use a coin as an analogy—heads or tails. However, the coin not only has two equal sides—it also has a rim that separates the two sides. The rim can be called the "middle ground" or "neutral dimension." Although the coin has two sides, it is a three-dimensional object. Three-dimensional thinking means stopping to consider this middle ground.

Human behavior, including things we think of as good and evil, are often perceived as having two equal and opposite sides. But in reality, these values fluctuate, expand, and shrink. They appear in different proportions in different times and different places or situations. It is easier to understand and explain good and evil by considering degrees and dimensions rather than polarities. When we use dimensions to describe positive, negative, and neutral human behavior by, we are considering not only black and white but also the shades of gray in between.

Three-dimensional thinking was practiced in the group discussions of my domestic violence prevention program. During the discussions, participants asked the following questions: Why does a good justice system seem unjust at times? Why does an honest, good person commit a brutal crime? Why does a good, generous, and loving partner become mean, cruel, barbaric, or even violent? Those questions point to the fact that people and organizations are never entirely good or evil.

Yet we want to believe our social systems are perfect and wholly good. When we learn that an innocent person has been serving time in jail, or that the police—defenders of the weak and innocent—engage in brutality, we are shocked and confused. We also want to believe that our leaders, including religious leaders and celebrities, are good. When we hear that someone in a position of trust has been involved in sexual misconduct, we become as frightened as when we hear that someone was killed violently and mercilessly by his or her own spouse. When we see people in terms of black and white, the gray shades in many situations surprise us. How could these things happen?

Three-dimensional thinking provides a way to help us understand human behavior more clearly. By using it, we will be able to resolve conflicts and problems faster and more effectively.

We become afraid or angry when the focus of our minds is on the negative dimension of an object, person, or situation. However, if we shift our focus from the negative dimension of a situation to the neutral and/or positive dimension of the same object, person, or situation, we will calm down very quickly.

Three Dimensions of Human Behavior

When astronauts go into space, they are able to clearly see Earth three dimensions and the effect its spherical shape has on daylight; they can see day on one side of the world, night on the other side, and twilight in between, all at the same time—something that we cannot see ourselves from Earth. Although these stages of the day seem to happen to us in a linear fashion when we are standing on Earth, what the astronauts see suggests that day, night, and twilight are one inseparable unit. They all exist at the same time when viewed from a distance.

Similarly, we can imagine the three-dimensional nature of human behavior—positive, negative, and neutral—generated by our mind, through what we choose to think. We display these behaviors in different proportions at different times and in different situations. When we view our behavior from a detached and distant perspective, we can see all of them clearly.

Positive Dimension: We can be happy, nice, gentle, kind, honest, caring, loving, compassionate, altruistic, and benevolent.

Negative Dimension: We can be angry, mean, selfish, deceptive, egotistical, threatening, terrorist, cruel, barbaric, and violent.

Neutral Dimension: We can be calm, relaxed, indifferent, inactive, unconcerned, and peaceful—as we are when we're asleep.

Here we are describing these behaviors in their most extreme states, forms, or qualities. We have a shortage of words in our language to accurately describe the exact quality, state, or intensity of a value. For example, the word "burn" is difficult to explain or understand without including the degrees of burn. The word "pain" is also difficult to explain or understand without using a number scale. Human emotion and behavior presents an even more difficult challenge to our vocabulary.

We tend to dichotomize good and evil. In a given situation, one's so-called good or evil behavior may fall between these two polarities, including right on the dividing line of neutrality. The qualities of good and evil can be more easily explained or understood if we consider that they also can be described in terms of percentage or degrees.

The Mind, a Super Power Generator

Many of us do not realize that our minds are a super power generator. Our thoughts, which can travel faster than the speed of light, are the fuel that runs the motor of our generator.

Our Creator has given us free will to choose our thoughts. We are free to shift our perceptions, which control our generator and generate the force that propels our behavior to reach our desired goals. Our positive thoughts produce positive forces and behaviors; our negative thoughts produce negative forces and behaviors. Our neutral thoughts generate only neutral behavior.

It is important to remember here that positive, negative, and neutral thoughts do not reflect the values of absolute good and evil. Here the system of positive, negative, and neutral is more closely analogous to the properties of electricity in an atom: the electron, proton, and neutron. For example, we might have the thought "I am hungry" or "I am full." The thought "I am hungry" might prompt us to reach for a dessert (a positive action), while the thought "I am full" might prompt us to decline a dessert that someone offers (a negative action). We also might feel neutral on the subject of the dessert, if we are neither hungry nor full. But being hungry is not good and being full is not evil.

We can control our behavior by utilizing appropriate thoughts of positive, negative, or neutral. Aesop's fable "The Fox and the Grapes" illustrates how this works.

> *Once up on a time, there was a fox wandering around in the farm in search of food. He saw the ripe, red grapes on the vine high over his head. He contemplated how delicious and juicy they would be to eat. He jumped up toward the grapes, but he could not reach them. Although he jumped up again and again, he could never reach them. Finally, he got tired of jumping, so he said to himself, "I think those grapes would taste sour anyway," and he walked away.*

Among other things, this story teaches us that we can change our thoughts and thereby change our feelings and behavior. We all know how to do it. However, when we are emotionally charged with greed, lust, or anger—our feelings are at high intensity. With our emotions going one hundred miles an hour, it becomes very difficult to stop or change our thoughts from negative to positive or from positive to negative. It would be easier to switch them from positive or negative to neutral first, before we shift them all the way into reverse. If we begin in a neutral position, the transition to negative or to positive occurs more smoothly. Neutral thinking slows down the speed and intensity of our emotional state and gives us an opportunity to make a better choice about our feelings and behavior.

Sometimes people feel stuck with one type of thought and behavior, unable to move in any direction—forward, backward or sideways—because they don't know how to or they forget to exercise their free will to choose better thoughts and change their feelings or behavior. Once we learn and practice the system of three-dimensional thinking, it becomes as easy to switch our thoughts as it is to shift our car into drive, reverse, or neutral.

Sexuality presents a particular challenge because our sexual urges are prompted by a strong drive. Walking away from a sexually enticing situation is often much harder than walking away from an offer to eat ripe grapes.

Positive mental forces tend to attract other positive forces and seek for integration or bonding together. This is why two individuals—whether the same sex or opposite sex—with positive mental force (passion) and perception about each other's values and interests tend to attract each other, a bond that may be called brotherly or sisterly love or "agape," a term that describes love that is not related to sexual desire.

When two individuals attract each other with unbridled positive mental force (passion) about each other's physical beauty (which includes the urge to touch, pet, caress, and explore the sensational experience of bonding with the other), they will have the urge to consummate sexual pleasure and have intercourse. We also call this love or the Greek term *eros*.

We must remember that love (agape) and lust (eros) are generated with the same positive mental force and perception but they are extremely different. If we care about adhering to religious moral values and/or professional ethical values, we need to be aware of our positive mental force (passion). We can control our sexual attraction by using neutral and or negative mental force and perception, we can give and receive love with co-workers, boss, clients, customers, and devotees of our religious organization without crossing the line into immoral or unethical conduct.

Most leaders are successful in controlling their sexual attraction and desire, unless they forget or choose to disregard their ethical values. It may be beneficial to future leaders if I share my personal experience in controlling the sexual attraction I have felt toward my clients and subordinates.

When I was in graduate school studying social work and clinical psychology, I learned how important it is to show empathy for my clients. During my internship and professional career, as I practiced empathy with my clients, I felt closer to them. When a female client showed her appreciation by taking my hand or hugging me, I felt aroused. but I remembered that it would be dangerous to violate my professional ethics. I used neutral thinking toward the behavior of my clients and I let my attractions dissolve without acting on them. Practice brings conditioning and conditioning makes our task easy.

Some of us find it difficult to distinguish between the negative and neutral dimensions of our behavior. We tend to see neutral as negative, but when we examine carefully, we see there is a difference between them—just as we see the difference between night and twilight. In some situations, we may see only two dimensions and have difficulties seeing the third dimension, but then it will appear, like a silver lining around the clouds. The dimensions and angles of the geometric graphs below may help us understand how our positive, negative, and neutral characteristics and behavior fluctuate in different proportions at different times and in different situations.

Three Dimentional Thinking
In Different Forms

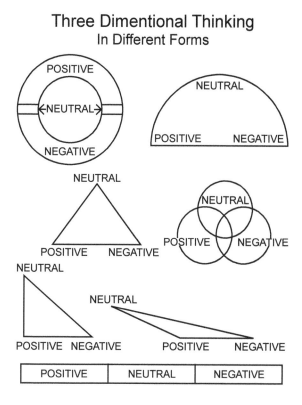

These three characteristics of human behavior have been described by Jesus Christ in the parable of the Good Samaritan: A man was traveling from Jerusalem to Jericho. On the way, robbers attacked him, stripped him of his clothes, and left him unconscious. A priest as well as a Levite came by on the same road; both saw the victim, but both passed to the other side. A Samaritan who was traveling on the same road saw the victim and felt compassion for him. He stopped, dressed the man's wounds, took him to an inn, and took care of him. The next day, the Samaritan gave money to the innkeeper to take care of the victim and promised to repay all expenses when he returned from his journey.

In this story, the Good Samaritan represents the positive, good nature of human behavior. The robbers represent the negative or bad nature of human behavior. The priest and Levite represent the neutral, indifferent nature of human behavior.

These three dimensions are not confined to human behavior. The things that we create also may have positive, negative, and neutral qualities. For instance, consider salt. Mild to moderate use of salt may help improve our health (positive dimension). Moderate to excessive use of it will damage our health (negative dimension). Salt is neither useful nor harmful when we do not use these products (neutral dimension).

For another example, consider nuclear weapons. They also have three dimensions: positive, negative, and neutral. The positive dimension is that they can be used for national safety and security. A nation that owns nuclear weapons can conquer its enemies easily with less manpower and fewer human casualties. The negative dimension of nuclear weapons is that they cost a lot of money to build, which can be a waste because countries may never use them. Also, they are dangerous to keep and maintain, and if there is an accident, it can kill thousands of people surrounding the weapon site and initiate a global crisis. The neutral dimension can exist when there is no use for nuclear weapons. Imagine seeing them. They are just a concept and do not need to be built.

Yet another example is the holiday of Christmas. A positive dimension of Christmas can be experiencing the excitement and joy of celebrating the birth of Jesus Christ. People share their joy and happiness by giving gifts to their friends and family members. A negative dimension is that the commercialization of the holiday pressures people to spend money. Many people experience anger or depression when they do not have enough money to purchase food, clothes, or gifts. Some may go into debt to celebrate Christmas; others may feel lonely or depressed when they do not have their friends or loved ones with them to celebrate. A neutral dimension is that Christmas is just another day for some people—without the religious and social implications. It's just December 25.

Three Dimensions of Human Life

Our lives also have three dimensions. Thinking in the positive dimension, one can say that life is a miracle and is precious. It is a joy to be alive. It is exciting and thrilling to be able to walk, run, and fly. Life is a delightful challenge, a game to play, a song to sing, and a history to make. It is an opportunity to choose the way we desire to live. Life can be full of promise when we believe that we will grow up, find a beautiful wife or a handsome husband, and enjoy our families. It also presents a challenge for us to discover the secrets of the universe. Life presents us with opportunities to be creative and fulfill our fantasies and imaginations.

Thinking in the negative dimension, one might say that life is full of sorrow and sufferings from sickness, disease, and old age. It is unfair that some people are born rich and some people are born poor. Some people are born with talents and some people are born with handicaps. We have to live with predators—not only mountain lions and microbes but also thieves, swindlers, terrorists, and murderers. Others might see life as boring and meaningless. Still others see nothing but the stress that can come with meeting life's daily demands. Thinking in the neutral dimension, one might say that life is for the moment. It is uncertain. We are born today and we may die tomorrow. We have no need to worry whether we live or die.

As you consider these different dimensions, I am not suggesting that that we must always think positive thoughts or that we should eradicate negative and neutral thinking from our lives. We must learn how to use positive, negative, AND neutral thinking for our benefit in the appropriate times, places, and situations.

Life can be like driving a car. While we are driving, we must pay attention to the traffic and the road in front of us. We must watch the side-view and rear-view mirrors; otherwise, we may cause an accident. In the same way, we must focus on the positive dimension of our lives but also be aware of the usefulness of the negative and neutral dimensions.

Three Types of People in Our Lives

People can also be classified as positive, negative, and neutral. The number of people who are positive or negative toward us may be very few in comparison to those who are neutral toward us. Positive people are those who love us, care for us, and support us emotionally or financially. Negative people are the people who compete with us, dislike us, or wish us misfortune. Neutral people are those whose attitude is neither positive nor negative toward us.

It must also be noted that people behave differently to different people. People who are positive to one person may be negative or neutral to another. People who are negative to one person may be positive or neutral to another. In an organization in which you are the president, the proportion of positive, negative, and neutral people will be different than in other environments. There may be more people who are positive toward you than negative or neutral because you are in a position of power.

In your family constellation, the proportion of positive, negative, and neutral people will depend on your relationships with those family members. For reasons we cannot identify people's behaviors toward us may change from time to time. However, if we understand the three-dimensional characteristics of human behavior, we will be less frustrated and angry because we will recognize that people are complex beings. The semi-circle below can be used to evaluate the positive, negative, and neutral people in our lives.

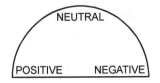

Fallible Employees and Employers

Even though we may be honest, faithful, and loyal to our employers, most of us have a boss or supervisor who monitors our job performance. Why do we need a supervisor or boss to check up on us? The reason is that it is possible for an honest, faithful, and loyal worker to fall into a neutral mode and become slothful or unproductive. He or she may also fall into negative mode and become destructive, which can be costly to the employer. It is unlikely that an employee will always perform positively.

If employers are absolutely one hundred percent just, honest, caring, reasonable, and law-abiding, why do we need labor unions? We need labor unions as well as bosses and supervisors because of our fallible human nature. Employees as well as employers are capable of positive, negative, and neutral behavior in different proportions depending on the place, time, and situation.

Fallible Husbands and Wives

It is possible for a loving and loyal husband or wife—or boyfriend or girlfriend—to slip into a neutral or negative mode and behave poorly. Ideally both individuals are equal partners, not detectives, or judges of each other. However, in many relationships, partners begin to blame and criticize one another.

When both partners are aware of the other's potential to behave positively, negatively and neutrally, they can help each other behave in helpful rather than hurtful ways.

Day, Night, and Twilight

As I said earlier, we cannot see the night when we are in the day or twilight. We cannot see the day while it is night or twilight. We cannot see the twilight when it is day or night. We must rise above the Earth like astronauts to see all three dimensions at the same time.

Similarly, we cannot see the positive when we are thinking about the negative and cannot see the negative while we are thinking about the positive. We sometimes cannot see neutral when we are thinking about positive or negative. The question arises: How can we see these three dimensions at the same time? The answer is that we must learn how to use the power of neutral thinking. We must learn to pull back, step aside, or rise above the problem in question—like an astronaut—by thinking in a neutral manner.

Neutral Thinking

We all know how to think positively and negatively, but many of us do not know how to think neutrally—or we are not accustomed to it. In addition, many of us are not aware of the power, effectiveness, and usefulness of neutral thinking.

Neutral thinking is a technique we can use to give rest to our mind. It gives us time to look for more options: fight (negotiation), flight (timeout), or freeze (acceptance). (Fight, flight, or freeze are explained in detail in the Chapter Three in the section titled "Understanding Our Stress.")

By thinking neutrally, we create the neutral dimension where there is no negativity or positivity. There is no war between good and evil. There is no anxiety, anger, longing, or joy. In neutrality, there is only peace and tranquility.

When we choose to be in the neutral dimension, we are able to temporarily detach ourselves from the world of tension, stress, and violence. Our negative thoughts and feelings become powerless and ineffective. We can be healed from our emotional wounds and regain emotional control. For example, when you are a referee between two competing teams in a game, you are placing yourself as a neutral person. As a referee, you are not concerned about any team's success or failure. No matter which team wins or loses, you will not be emotionally affected, because your feelings about them will be neutral.

Neutral thinking has its drawbacks. Prolonged neutral thinking toward our creativity and material progress may keep us idle or unproductive in our lives. On the other hand ongoing neutral thinking about betraying a friend, stealing, or using drugs can help us stay resist these temptations, which can be a positive influence in our lives.

Essentially, neutral thinking is similar to sleep. Enough sleep is necessary for our bodies to rest, but sleeping for the rest of our lives is not desirable.

Steps to Enter into the Neutral Dimension

Your mind is the fastest vehicle on the planet. Your memory and imagination can take you from your first kiss to your current job crisis instantaneously. In the neutral dimension you can focus of any event, situation, object, or person within seconds by using the following steps:

Step One: Acknowledge the event, situation, object, or person.

Step Two: Release the physical tension, if any, in your body by breathing deeply.

Step Three: Think neutral thoughts by asking yourself these questions: "Do I have all the information about this event, situation, object, or person? Do I need this event, situation, object, or person in my life? Can I survive without this event, situation, object, or person? What are the proportions or degrees of positive, negative, and neutral dimensions of this event, situation, object, or person in my life?" By answering these neutral questions, you enter into the neutral dimension.

Energy and Magnetic Field

We know that there are radio waves in the air around us even though we cannot see them. However, some of us are unaware of the energy and magnetic fields that we generate with our super power generators, because we cannot see the fields with our eyes. When we focus on the negative dimension of our lives, we may feel frightened, angry, or hostile. Our bodies produce adrenaline and cortisol as well as mild- to high-voltage negative energy, which create a negative magnetic field around us that repels other people as well as resources away from us.

Negative energy is generated by negative thinking. Negativity is more powerful than the positive energy in our bodies. It is high-voltage energy, like an atom bomb that can destroy anything and everything in its surroundings. We experience this energy when we are angry or stressed.

Most of the time, negative energy is undesirable because it distorts our thinking and hampers our judgment. For example, when someone is angry it might seem appropriate and reasonable to punch a hole in the wall or hurl an object at someone. We think this way only when we are highly stressed or angry.

When we are in the negative dimension, we are more likely to respond to a person, object, or event in a negative manner. When we respond to the world in a negative manner, the world tends to treat us negatively.

But when we focus on the positive dimension of our lives, our bodies produce endorphins and positive energy, creating a positive magnetic field around us, which attracts other people and resources to us. We become eager to discover the mysteries of the universe. We are willing to learn whatever it takes to be creative. We see our work as a source of pleasure rather than as a burden.

Positive energy is produced by positive thinking. This energy is less powerful than negative energy, but like a guided missile, it can hit a target precisely. Positive energy is desirable and more effective in problem solving and responding to threats that its inverse. Positive energy also enhances our reasoning, logic, and intuition. If we respond to the world in a positive manner, the world tends to treat us positively, helping us reach our goals.

When we focus our mind on the neutral dimension of our lives, we go into a rest mode. When we think neutral thoughts, our bodies rest from generating extra energy. Our bodies and minds experience peace and serenity. Our minds disengage from the positive or negative magnetic forces. Doing this allows us to **step back, step aside, or rise above** the issue in question. It puts us in the same position as the astronauts who see the Earth's three phases of light at the same time.

We can use our brains to protect us from harsh and dangerous environments, to provide our needs and wants in life, and to imagine possibilities. We can discover and invent things that enhance our comfort and happiness. Our mind can be an ally for creating joy, or it can be an enemy that creates miseries and unhappiness. It can also be neutral—neither ally nor enemy.

Neutral thinking helps us rise above a situation like a helium balloon. We learn to scan the positive, negative, and neutral dimensions before we decide what to do. A photographer uses similar techniques with his camera. He zooms in to get a close-up of a specific detail, but then he zooms out to get the whole, big picture.

There may come a time when you are contemplating a big decision, such as buying a home, getting married, filing for divorce, or signing on to a new business venture. When you have a decision to make, gather information from the three dimensions and make a decision based on what will produce the greatest number of positive possible outcomes for you. By approaching decisions in this Way, you are less likely to be confused. And if things do not go as planned or others disappoint you, three-dimensional thinking will help you deal with these stressors. **Strategies about how to do this are explained in detail in Chapter Three in the section titled "Understanding Our Stress."**

Summary

1. All events, objects, and situations have positive, negative, and neutral dimensions in different proportions.

2. All people have the potential capability to behave in a positive, negative, or neutral manner in different proportions, times, places, and situations.

3. Positive thoughts produce endorphins in our bodies that generate positive energy and create a positive magnetic field around us, which attracts people and resources towards us.

4. Negative thoughts produce adrenaline and cortisol in our bodies, which generate negative energy and create a negative magnetic field around us. Negative thoughts repel people and resources away from us.

5. Neutral thoughts do not generate positive or negative energy in our bodies, resulting in no magnetic field around us. Our bodies and minds rest in peace and serenity. When we are in the neutral dimension, it becomes easy for us to rise above a situation. Once we learn to evaluate all three dimensions, we can make better choices about our actions.

Questions

1. What is three-dimensional thinking?
2. What are the causes of our suffering?
3. Why do we sometimes see police brutality?
4. Why does a kind and loving person become mean and cruel to his or her spouse?
5. Why do celebrities as well as political and religious leaders get involved in sexual misconduct?
6. What are three-dimensional human behaviors?
7. How does one think neutral thoughts?
8. What are our energy and magnetic fields and how do they work?

Exercises

1. Write down one of your concerns, problems, or desires.
2. Write down the neutral aspects, effects, or qualities of the identified concern, problem, or desire.
3. Write down the positive aspects, effects, or qualities of the identified concern, problem, or desire.
4. Write down the negative aspects, effects, or qualities of the identified concern, problem, or desire.

5. Evaluation: Check which dimension provides the highest percentage or degree of good, advantage, or benefit for you.

CHAPTER THREE

SKILLS AND STRATEGIES

Stress

"Stress is tax you pay for not taking one hundred percent responsibility for your life." — Dr. Barnet Meltzer

We all know what excessive stress can do to our physical and mental energy. What can we do to manage our stress levels and simultaneously increase our energy? There are many resources available—such as yoga, meditation, relaxation techniques, and sauna baths—that can help us release physical and mental tension. While all of these activities are good for our health, if we recognize the root cause of our stress, we can instantaneously be free of stress in seconds. The real cause of our stress is our dislike of things, people, places, and situations. It "is the seed that then grows like a tree within us, by degrees.

If we eliminate the very birth of our stress and never plant the seed, we will increase our physical and mental energy. If we manage our stress level, we can prevent the biological stress defense mechanisms of "fight, flight, or freeze" by preventing the very first onset of an unpleasant experience.

A modified version of "fight, flight, or freeze" is "negotiation, timeout, or acceptance." Because we have free wills, we can choose one of the latter three; when we do, we will prevent harmful stress.

UNDERSTANDING OUR STRESS

We talk about how hectic and stressful our daily lives are in this constantly evolving industrial society. Stress may cause us to experience physical symptoms such as stomach ulcers, tension headaches, skin rashes, insomnia, backaches, as well as shoulder and neck pains. We may try to overcome these symptoms by using alcohol, illicit drugs, or over-the-counter drugs such as sleeping pills and painkillers—all of which can cause more problems than they solve.

When we get a promotion or get fired from our job, we experience stress. When we get married or divorced, we feel stressed. Whether we have to work or go on vacation, we feel stressed. We experience stress in response to sad as well as happy occasions.

We feel stressed not only from current events but also from past and future events. We may suffer from the post-traumatic stress of a rape, a car accident, or wrongful treatment in childhood. We experience anxiety from upcoming events such as weddings, socialization parties, holidays, job promotions, job loss, exams, and performances. We also experience stress while watching television programs that give details about wars, crimes, famine, terrorist threats, and corruption—even though we are not directly involved. However, what is stressful to one person is not necessarily stressful to another. Two people can experience the same event and each may feel differently about it. Therefore, it is very important what shapes how we feel.

Three Dimensions of Stress

Dr. Hans Selye, known for his pioneering research on stress, demonstrated that stress has different meanings to different people. He explained that stress equals distress. An event, person, situation, virus, or environment may play a supportive role as a stressor, but **our negative perceptions, negative interpretations, and negative beliefs about them are mainly responsible for our stress.** Stress may contain positive, negative, and neutral dimensions in different proportions.

Positive Dimension: Stress can help us function at our optimum level to increase productivity and bring joy to our lives.

Negative Dimension: Stress can cause irritability, tension, neck pain, ulcers, anxiety, depression, or heart attack. **Neutral Dimension:** Stress can be in a dormant or inactive state. It can be neutralized by neutral thinking.

This wide range of possible responses explains why the same event can elicit excitement in some people, anxiety in others, and virtually no reaction in others.

Suppose you are satisfied and happy with your present job and you get a promotion. The new promotion will place you on new job performance probation for six months. If you focus on the positive dimension of the job promotion, you will perceive and interpret it positively. Your body generates endorphins. You will see it as a challenge and an opportunity for your career advancement. If you focus on the negative dimension of the job promotion, your body will produce adrenaline and cortisol. You may feel the threat of losing your present job and the risk of taking the job promotion. When you focus on the neutral dimension of the job promotion, you will perceive and interpret it as neutral. Your body and mind remain in rest mode. You may say to yourself, "Today, I got a promotion, and tomorrow I may get a demotion." You will feel neither worried nor excited.

Suppose that you have been employed at your job for three years and your employer fires you for unsatisfactory job performance. If you focus on the neutral dimension of the job loss, you will perceive and interpret it as neutral. Your body and mind will remain in rest mode. You may say to yourself: "This is not the only job in the world. I can survive without this job." You may feel neither worried nor excited. If you focus on the negative dimension of the job loss, you will perceive and interpret it as negative. You may say to yourself: "I was fired; no one is going to hire me ever again. I am not good enough. Something is wrong with me." Your body produces adrenaline and cortisol. You may feel shocked, unjustly treated, and angry—all very stressful emotions. When you focus on the positive dimension of the job loss your body generates endorphins. You may say to yourself: "I will find a better job. This is an opportunity." You may feel excited to find a better job that would be more satisfying or take a vacation.

Our negative perception and interpretation of an event, object, person, or situation may become our perceived threat to our existence. When we perceive a threat, our bodies produce adrenaline from adrenal cortex and cortisol from hypothalamus, warning us that there is something wrong or dangerous and that we need to protect ourselves. Our digestive system slows down, and blood rushes to our muscles and brain. Our breathing gets faster, our heart rate speeds up, and our blood pressure increases. We may feel increased perspiration, and our muscles may contract. When we respond neutrally to the signal, the adrenaline, cortisol, and negative energy subside and we feel relieved. But when we do not respond with appropriate defense strategies and continue stewing, brooding, or dwelling on our negative thoughts, we continue producing adrenaline and cortisol and emitting negative energy, causing our stress level to increase even further. If the stress continues to escalate, an anxiety attack, major depression, a heart attack, or a stroke may follow.

Fight, Flight, and Freeze

When animals are threatened or perceive a threat, they fight, flee, or freeze. Similarly, when humans are involved in warfare, we fight, retreat, or surrender. These three responses are automatic physiological defense mechanisms designed to help us survive.

Today, there are many tribes and primitive societies around the world that use fight, flight, and freeze stress reactions for their survival. People who live in tree houses in New Guinea, the Serengeti and the Amazon jungle live under the law of survival of the fittest, where "might is right."

In our advanced and civilized society, fight, flight, and freeze are often not useful responses. However, these instinctual responses can always be useful if we reframe them. The difference between animals and humans is that animals react to perceived threats, whereas humans can learn concepts and skills that can inform and change their responses.   Rather than physically hurting or verbally accosting each other, we can address our differences in a more thoughtful way. The fight response can be reframed as a **negotiation**, or the act of facing the issue in question by discussing, coming to a mutual agreement, and resolving the conflict with respect and honor. The **flight** response can be reframed as a **timeout**—an opportunity to walk away in order to escape or avoid violence. Rather than **freeze,** we humans can **accept**, surrender, or comply. There are times when, if we wish to guarantee our own well-being and safety, we must submit our will and obey.

Life is for living, and living is a challenge. If we want to live and enjoy, we must respond to that challenge. It is a challenge to get food, clothes, a house, a car, a good-paying job, and a companion. We must focus on the positive dimension and view our lives as an opportunity for enjoyment and fulfillment, not as a threat or punishment.

When we are in an unavoidable conflict and we do not resolve by responding appropriately, we will likely experience stress that produces adrenalin and cortisol and distorts our thinking. The negative energy that such a response produces repels other people and resources away from us. We may feel stuck, confused, or frustrated. Given the effect these emotions have on our ability to think clearly, it is wise to respond with appropriate defense strategies: negotiation, timeout, or acceptance.

Steps to Deal with Stress

Whenever we don't like something or something we may perceive it as a threat and experience emotional as well as physical tension. We can overcome these stressful feelings by using the following steps:

Step One: Shift our focus from the negative dimension of a situation to its neutral dimension. Neutral thinking allows us to momentarily doubt our perception of stress. When the perceived stress is questionable, our fear and anger naturally subside. Our hypothalamus and adrenal cortex stop secreting cortisol and adrenalin, and the high-voltage negative energy will be turned off. The negative magnetic field around us disappears. We then are able to calm ourselves down and gain emotional control.

Step Two: Shift your focus of mind from the neutral dimension to the positive dimension of your situation. When we do this, our bodies start generating endorphins and positive energy, creating a positive magnetic field around us. The positive energy enhances our logic, reasoning, and intuition. The positive magnetic field attracts other people and resources. We then are able to re-evaluate the situation with our positive energy, and take appropriate action strategies.

Step Three: Choose one of the three defense strategies: **negotiation**, **timeout**, or **acceptance**. Once we respond to the perceived threat appropriately, we recover from our stressful feelings and can once again enjoy life.

For example, suppose you are driving your car on the freeway and suddenly someone pulls his car in front of you and slams on his brakes. You **notice his inappropriate behavior.** You may feel irritated or angry. If you think negatively towards him for more than ten seconds, your adrenaline will spread throughout your body. You may say to yourself, "What an inconsiderate driver! He just missed causing an accident." You may start honking, shouting, calling him names, showing a fist or finger. You may also carry that anger to your job or family, which may cause you more problems. If you think neutrally towards the driver, your adrenaline rush will cease and you will feel at ease. You may say to yourself, "It does not matter; I am not in a hurry, and I am safe." **(Acceptance)** You will be able to remain calm and cool. However, if you think positively about the incident, you may change your lane and drive at the speed you desire. **(Timeout)** The Negotiation response does not apply in this incident.

Dealing with Freeway Stress

Imagine that you are on the freeway driving your car to work. There has been an accident so the traffic is backed up. Your speedometer shows you are going five to ten miles an hour. You are worried about being late to work or being fired from your job. In this stressful situation, what options do you have? **Negotiate? Take a timeout? Or accept?** You cannot discuss and negotiate with anyone in a traffic jam. You cannot take a physical timeout, but you can take a mental timeout. The other choice you have is acceptance. Accept the traffic condition. Think about other things. To reduce your feelings of stress, frame it in a neutral or positive way: an accident can happen to anybody. It could have happened to me. I am safe. I am glad that I am not involved in that accident.

Dealing with Job Stress

Suppose that you are employed at a company where you have to work different shifts—day, swing, and night. Because of your unpredictable work schedule, you cannot make plans to spend time with your spouse and children. Your spouse and children miss your company. When you come home from work, they are often not at home or they are asleep. You cannot afford to quit the job because you have the responsibility of paying the mortgage, car payment, and other bills. You experience stress and feel trapped about your work schedule. You also feel helpless and hopeless. What are the choices you have in this situation? **Fight=negotiate? Or flight=take timeout? Or freeze=accept?** You may choose to discuss your family situation with your boss and negotiate for a regular shift. You may take the second choice and find another job that fits your desired family lifestyle. If you decide not to discuss the issue with your boss or look for another job, you have a third option: acceptance. You accept the fact that your work schedule is unpredictable and ask your family to spend time with you when you are available. In order to get relief from stress, you take your focus off the negative dimension and place it on the positive dimension of your job and family: I have a good job, and I can spend quality time with my family. If we plan well, I can have both.

Dealing with Marital Stress

Suppose you have been married for ten years. You have three children ages nine, seven, and five. During the past two years, your marital relationship has become unsatisfactory. Your spouse spends money on his or her personal luxuries and you have the responsibility of paying the bills and providing all the family necessities. Your spouse does not appreciate what you do for the family. When you attempt to communicate with your spouse, he or she gets angry with you. You feel helpless and trapped **Fight=negotiate? Or flight=take timeout? Or freeze=accept?** Accepting the unsatisfactory relationship does not seem to be a good choice. Timeout or divorce may be the last resort. If you choose to discuss your grievances with your partner and negotiate in a civilized manner, you will have the ability to focus on the positive dimension of your relationship. Your body will start producing endorphins, which in turn create positive energy, allowing you to reason clearly and find a solution to resolve the problem.

Using "I messages" will help a negotiation be successful. "I messages" are telling the other person **how you feel**, rather than what he or she is doing wrong to you. Instead of saying "You are making me crazy" say "I feel angry." Instead of saying "How dare you humiliate me?" say "I feel humiliated and hurt when you call me names." Telling the other person how you feel gives him or her the chance to re-evaluate his or her behavior. Do not blame, accuse, intimidate, or threaten your partner while discussing your feelings and conflicts. Remember that you cannot get love and support from a person whom you condemn and criticize. You must validate his or her feelings and concerns with love. If you and your partner cannot resolve the conflicts, you may consider seeking professional help.

Summary

1. Stress is a neurophysiologic response. An event, person, situation, illness, or environment may play influence the response, but **our negative perceptions, interpretations, and beliefs are primarily responsible for our stress.**

2. Stress has three dimensions: positive, negative, and neutral. We feel positive, negative, or neutral according to our perceptions and interpretations.

3. If we focus on the neutral dimension of the stressor, we will perceive and interpret it as neutral. Our bodies and minds will remain in the rest mode, helping us stay calm and in control.

4. Fight, flight, and freeze are physiological defense responses to perceived threats. In the three-dimensional thinking paradigm they are reframed as negotiation, timeout, and acceptance, respectively, and are used as defense strategies to deal with stress.

When we perceive a threat or dislike something, we have the choice to respond with one of the three defense strategies: **(1) fight=negotiation** (facing the issue, discussing, and compromising) **(2) flight=timeout** (taking a short or long timeout, walking away, avoiding, and escaping) **(3) freeze=acceptance** (acknowledging or complying).

Questions

1. What is stress?
2. What are the three dimensions of stress?
3. What are the fight, flight, and freeze responses?
4. What steps deal effectively with stress?

SECTION TWO

ANGER

Anger is an emotional reaction of extreme displeasure and suggests neither a degree of intensity nor an outward manifestation. Some synonyms for anger are rage, fury, indignation, and wrath. Rage implies a loss of self-control that can lead to violence. Fury suggests even more violence and connotes a degree of temporary madness. Indignation connotes righteous anger at what one considers unfair or shameful. Wrath, closely linked rage and indignation, suggests an intent to avenge or punish.

Anger might be easier to understand if there were some of measuring it as we do a fever, but unfortunately there is no such devise. We tend to use the word "anger" for all categories of harsh negative feelings. Annoyance and indignation are lesser degrees of anger, which can be less harmful to self and others. Rage and fury are higher degrees of anger that can be more harmful to self and others. Wrath is a word for anger we seldom use in day-to-day life.

What makes us happy, angry or neither? This question has been asked again and again. Does one thousand dollars make you happy, angry, or neither? Does your partner make you happy, angry, or neither? Does name-calling make you happy, angry, or neither? What about sex? What about work? The answers to these questions depend on your likes, dislikes, or neutral feelings regarding the people or situations in question.

Common Causes of Anger

The common cause of our anger is our disliking things, persons, situations, and events. Our disliking is based on our thinking. In a given moment, there is no way we would ever get angry about persons and situations we like. We feel uncomfortable or upset only when we dislike something. It could be something we want and we don't have or something given to us that we don't want. If we do not like our job, the thought of going to work may make us angry, but when we like our job, going to work may be exciting. During conversations, if we like what our partner says to us, it can prompt a night of romance, but if we do not like what our partner says to us we may become angry. When we do not like what someone does or says to us and react by getting angry. The better way is to choose your response. Animals tend to react when they dislike something, but we humans have the ability to think before we act.

If we do not respond appropriately or try to ignore our negative response, our bodies continue secreting adrenalin and cortisol, both of which cause confusion and poor judgment. A high level of anger may cause anxiety and depression, which may lead to destructive behavior.

Three Dimensions of Anger

When we read and compare the meanings of the synonyms of anger, we find the three inherent qualities positive, negative, and neutral in different proportions. We call anger a negative emotion because it has more negative elements than positive and neutral ones.

Positive Dimension: The positive characteristic of anger is that it warms us up, gives us energy, and motivates us to take action when something goes wrong or something happens we dislike.

Negative Dimension: The negative characteristic of anger is that it can overheat our bodies and minds. It creates confusion and emotional turmoil. Under its influence, we may become furious, enraged, violent, and destructive.

Neutral Dimension: Anger, like any emotion, can be neutralized by neutral thinking.

The three dimensions of anger can be better understood by using the following triangle.

In the above triangle, the negative angle is larger than the positive or neutral angles. The negative consequences of anger outweigh more than the positive or neutral. Therefore, anger is mainly considered a negative emotion.

How Do We Get Angry?

Our interpretation of stimuli gives birth to our emotions. A stimulus can be any number of things such as an object, event, or person. In the universe, all stimuli have three dimensions: positive, negative, and neutral in various proportions. When we see and interpret positive aspects about a person, object, or event, we feel good or happy. When we see and interpret negative aspects about them, we feel bad or angry. When we see and interpret neutrally about them, we feel neither happy nor angry.

In order to understand how we get angry, it may be helpful to make a comparison with how cars get overheated. If we understand our car's heating and cooling system, we can prevent it from getting overheated by checking its parts regularly. If we don't understand how these systems work, then we wouldn't do anything until it overheats. To prevent such as problem, we read our car manual and learn how to maintain our car properly.

Do you know how your mind and body get overheated when you get angry? You may say, "My boss, customers, co-workers, and spouse push my buttons and make me angry." Do you think this is true? You may answer, "Yes." Are you a puppet or robot with strings or buttons that people can push or pull any time to make you jump up or fall down? Think about it. If other people have access to your strings or buttons, that means you do not have any control over yourself. You behave as other people make you behave. This is erroneous thinking.

Our Creator has given us free will to make choices in our lives. We choose to interpret the stimuli in our environment; in turn these interpretations shape our emotions. No matter what other people are doing or what the situation is, our responses are shaped by how we interpret and perceive, not by the stimuli themselves. **No one makes us angry; our negative thoughts, interpretations, and beliefs do.** We are responsible for our thoughts, feelings, and behaviors.

For example, imagine that you are visiting a small town in India. You are walking in your host's backyard, and suddenly you see a big tiger coming toward you. Would you go and pet him, run away, fight him, or freeze? You will behave according to what you think in your mind. If you think yourself strong enough, you might put up a fight. If you think the tiger will attack and eat you, you may run for your life. If you think that you cannot run away or fight, you may freeze. If you think that the tiger is your host's pet, you might be glad to touch and pet him.

Imagine that you are at Sunset Beach in Hawaii. You love water but do not know how to swim or surf. You get into two feet of water and see a ten-foot wave coming toward you. What goes through your mind? You may think that the wave is going to drown you, and that thought makes you afraid. People who know how to swim and surf may be happy to see the big wave because they think of having fun in it.

Envision a rattlesnake coming toward you. Would you be happy, scared, or carefree? What would go through your mind?

You have the choice to interpret the snake as negative, positive, or neutral. A negative interpretation might be that it is venomous and therefore dangerous. A positive interpretation could be that its skin can be used to make expensive boots and that its meat is delicious. A neutral interpretation could be that if you yield to him there is no danger and you do not care for its skin or meat.

So, it is not the tiger, the big wave, or the rattlesnake that make you feel afraid. It is your negative perceptions and thoughts about them.

Suppose that you love to eat pickles. Now, close your eyes and think about pickles. In a few seconds, your mouth will water and you will taste them. How did this happen? There is no real pickle in front of you. It is only your thinking that caused your body's chemicals and your feelings to change.

Imagine that it is your birthday. Your partner presents a beautiful cake to you. When you see the cake, what goes through your mind? Do you think positive, negative, or neutral thoughts? How do you feel? Do you feel happy, unhappy, or neither? Most of us will think positive thoughts about the cake as well as about our partner's behavior, and we may feel happy. Suppose that as you are enjoying your first bite of cake, your partner says that the cake was given to him or her from his or her ex-boyfriend or ex–girlfriend. When you hear this information, what goes through your mind? As in the other examples, the stimulus, the cake in this instance, was not the reason for your happiness or unhappiness. It was your thoughts about the cake and the thoughts about our partner's behavior that made us feel happy, unhappy, or neither.

Now you can see that it is not your boss, customers, co-workers, and partner that make you mad. It is your negative perception of the person and his or her behavior. So, if you would like to stop getting mad and instead gain and maintain full emotional control of yourself, all you have to do is focus on the neutral dimension of the object, person, or event in question. Neutral thinking brings peace and serenity in your body and mind. When you think neutral, your mind and body go to rest. Once you have calmed down and are no longer angry, focus on the positive dimension of that object, person, or event to resolve the problem at hand.

Now you know what makes you angry. In our day-to-day lives, when we run into negative incidents or negative thoughts, we can feel sparks of anger. It is like accidentally placing our fingers on a hot stove. If we pull our fingers out immediately, we may feel the extreme heat, but our fingers might not get burned. However, if we keep our fingers on a hot stove for five seconds or longer, our fingers will get burned. Similarly, fifteen seconds or a longer duration of anger causes our minds and bodies to start getting overheated, and we may be on the verge of getting furious or enraged.

Prolonged anger is generated by focusing on negative thoughts, interpretations, or beliefs. If we do it long enough, we can become like monsters, and nobody can stop us from our destructive behavior. In order to prevent ourselves from coming to that point, we must learn to recognize our physiological symptoms such as increased heart rate, muscle tension, loud tone of voice, and increased body temperature. When we experience any of these physical symptoms, we must take a "time out" and shift the focus of our minds from the negative dimension to the neutral dimension of that object, person, or event. By doing so, we can defuse or refrain from getting furious, enraged, or violent.

You may say that you become violent instantly—that there is no time to think or observe your own physiological symptoms. In this case, your violent behavior has become a conditioned, addictive behavior. Section Three—**Understanding Our Habits and Addiction,** in Chapter Three will explain how this happens and what to do about it.

Summary

We behave the way it makes sense to us at any given moment. Generally, we don't do crazy things knowing they are wrong. Even if we do crazy things, they make perfect sense to us at a particular time. All events, objects, people's behavior, and situations have positive, negative, and neutral dimensions in various proportions. We see the world through the lens of our memories and interpret the events, situations, objects, and people as they make sense to us. It is necessary for every one of us to enhance the power of our memory lens by refining our perceptions and analytical abilities so that we interpret the world more accurately.

What is anger? Anger is a strong feeling of displeasure or antagonism. The common cause of anger is our disliking things, persons, situations, and events. Our disliking is based on our thinking. Anger has three dimensions—positive, negative, and neutral—and is aroused by our negative thinking. The way we perceive something determines whether we feel happy, unhappy, or angry. We are solely responsible for our thoughts, feelings, and behaviors.

Questions

1. What is anger?
2. What is the common cause of anger?
3. What are the three dimensions of anger?
4. How do we get angry?
5. How can we reduce and release our anger?

UNDERSTANDING OUR HABITS AND ADDICTIONS

We are evaluated by our employers, bosses, customers, and friends regarding our tendencies and habits, which include our reliability, punctuality, honesty, and trustworthiness. Our credit ratings are based on our purchasing and payment habits. Many lucrative businesses such as breweries, fast food chains, liquor stores, and credit card companies flourish due to human habits. All humans desire pleasure and aim to avoid pain. We like to do things that give us an experience of positive feelings and to avoid things that give us pain or negative feelings. According to *Webster's Dictionary*, an addiction is a habitual or obsessive behavior, much like devotion. The components of a habit are addiction, **training, education, conditioning, programming, and practice,** all of which require a specific repeated behavior. Habits are necessary because they simplify our lives and increase our productivity. Most of us routinely get out of bed, use the restroom, brush our teeth, take a shower, dress, eat our breakfast, and go to work on time. Otherwise, we would be late and unable to keep our jobs. Without forming positive habits, we would not be successful in our professions.

Researchers say that it takes a minimum of twenty-one times to form a habit. We can choose our habits and discontinue them if we wish. However, over time, habits can become addictions. An addiction is a powerful subconscious behavior. At times, it seems uncontrollable and unstoppable. Subconscious behavior takes place when our bodies do something without the awareness of our conscious minds. For example, you may be driving a car on the freeway and busy thinking about something else with your conscious mind, not paying attention to where you are going, and you drive your car to your work or home, or another unintended place. Another example is that you may be parking your car in a particular parking space and one time you find that someone else parked his car in that space. You end up having to park your car somewhere else. When you return to your car, your body walks to your regular parking space, and you may be surprised that your car is not there. A sudden thought may flash in your mind that your car might be stolen. But immediately, you realize that you did not park your car in that parking space. Then your conscious mind leads you to the parking space where you parked. Subconscious behavior is beneficial to most basketball players, boxing champions, musicians, and dancers. They acquire this behavior intentionally by conditioning, programming, and practicing to succeed in achieving their goals.

Three Dimensions of Habits and Addictions

Habits and addictions have three dimensions: positive, negative, and neutral in different proportions.

Positive Dimension: Habits can help us succeed in achieving our desired goals and may bring joy to our lives. An addiction may function similarly, helping us perform well, at least temporarily, in our chosen field. One can be habituated or addicted to save money and become rich. One can be habituated or addicted to learning and become a professional or a specialist in his or her chosen field. One can be habituated or addicted to walking, jogging, weight lifting, and maintaining good physical health.

Negative Dimension: Habits of drinking alcohol, cigarette smoking, illicit drug use, overeating, tardiness, or using profanity are undesirable in our society. Addictions to alcohol and illegal drugs may cause one to suffer from poor health and loss of a job or family. You can be habituated or addicted to anger and violence and may suffer from litigations and rejections by others. One can be habituated or addicted to spending money and may live in debt. One can be habituated or addicted to gambling and may live in poverty or lose his or her family.

Neutral Dimension: Habits and addictions have a dormant state. Many people are free from alcohol and substance abuse. Habits and addictions can be neutralized by neutral thinking about the substance, products, or items involved. (See "Steps to enter into neutral dimension" in Chapter Two.)

The Subcategory Positive Addiction also has three dimensions: positive, negative, and neutral in different proportions. For example, if you are addicted to saving money you might gain financial security and win the respect of others. But if you neglect your health or ignore your family because of the addiction, it is a tragedy. Ideally you would learn to balance your behavior of saving money by using the triangle below:

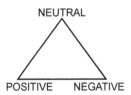

NEUTRAL

POSITIVE   NEGATIVE

Place the positive aspects of saving money in the positive angle. Place the negative aspects of saving money in the negative angle. By having neutral thoughts about saving money, you will be able to control or balance your addiction in order to enjoy your health, wealth, and family.

How Habits and Addictions Are Formed

It is important to understand how we form habits and addictions. Genetics, personality, and environmental factors play a role in forming addictions. An individual's positive perceptions, interpretations, and feelings towards a stimulus and the association of that stimulus with pleasure are essential components. When we perceive a stimulus, we respond positively, negatively, or neutrally according to our perceptions and interpretations. If we have positive perceptions and interpretations, we experience positive feelings and associate those feelings with that substance, person or activity with pleasure—driving us to want more. If we have negative perceptions and interpretations, we experience negative feelings, and have associations with the substance, object, person, or event. These feelings become painful, and we dislike, avoid, hate, or eliminate them as we eliminate spiders or roaches in our homes. If we respond with neutral perceptions and interpretations, we experience neutral feelings associated with that substance, object, person, or event, resulting in an unaffected emotional state. We remain unconcerned, calm, and at ease. It is clear that we cannot form a habit or be addicted to a stimulus when we perceive, interpret, and experience neutral.

Addictions to Substances

When we taste coffee, alcohol, or smoke a cigarette for the first time, it is not pleasant. Yet, after a few minutes we may feel relaxed, amused, or at ease. Thus, we associate the taste of coffee, alcohol, or cigarette smoking with positive feelings and pleasure. Then we consciously choose coffee, alcohol, or smoking cigarettes. We willingly accept the little pain of unpleasant taste for the greater pleasure. Gradually, our coffee, alcohol, or nicotine of cigarette usage progresses from conscious to subconscious behavior. We use it compulsively and without awareness. We use alcohol, cigarette smoking, or illicit drugs for social fun. If we like it, we associate that substance with pleasure. Once we are addicted to any substance such as coffee, alcohol, cigarettes, or drugs, our behavior becomes very powerful, even uncontrollable. We may feel powerless, helpless, and hopeless and see no way out.

Many people have convinced themselves that addiction is destructive or harmful to them or others and quit their habit without professional help. However, some individuals who are addicted to alcohol, cigarette smoking, or other substances may need a medical evaluation to ensure that they are physically and emotionally stable before they start practicing three-dimensional thinking.

Once you start behaving without awareness, you may have difficulty stopping the substance abuse with only willpower. You may need a supportive environment such as rehabilitation center or halfway house for your recovery. When you try to avoid the substance that you are addicted to, you will struggle, especially when you are exposed to it.

You are addicted to the alcohol, cigarettes, or other substance because of your positive perceptions, interpretations, and feelings associated with pleasure. Your addiction blinds you to the negative consequences. Focusing on the neutral dimension of the substance allows you to detach yourself and see all three dimensions.

In the neutral dimension, there is no positive force that will pull you back. You will be able to disengage yourself from the positive dimension of the substance and or rise above it—like astronauts— to see your own condition. If you are in a twelve-step program or under medical treatment for substance abuse, continue your treatment and practice three-dimensional thinking as well.

By thinking neutral, you will remove the tension and struggle from your consciousness. Your cravings for the substance will diminish. You will feel at ease and calm. You will be able to see clearly both the positive and negative outcomes of the substance use. It will become easier for you to control your addiction or choose to be free from it. This process is similar to your car transmission. Once your car is in drive, it cannot go to reverse directly without a struggle; it has to go through neutral. The neutral helps to disengage from drive or reverse. Similarly, neutral thinking will help you disengage yourself from positive or negative thinking about the substance in question. It will help you to see and evaluate both the positive and negative consequences of substance abuse. You will be able to make a better choice. Remember, nobody can stop or change your behavior of substance abuse except you. (See Chapter Two "Steps to Enter into the Neutral Dimension.")

Steps to Overcoming Cigarette Smoking

Cigarette smoking is a worldwide human health problem. Smoking induces a moment of euphoria followed by depression. It has three-dimensional effects, positive, negative, and neutral. Taking the following steps will help you quit cigarette smoking:

Step One: Take a neutral stance about cigarette smoking by asking yourself these questions: "Do I have to smoke cigarettes?" "Can I survive without it?" "Can I get others' opinions including my loved ones about whether I should smoke cigarettes?"

Step Two: Make three separate lists of the positive, negative, and neutral consequences of cigarette smoking.

Step Three: Keep the list of the negative consequences of cigarette smoking on an index card and carry it with you.

Step Four: Read the consequences to yourself as often as possible, especially when you feel tempted by opportunity for smoking cigarettes.

Step Five: Associate smoking cigarettes with the pain or negative consequences you have already experienced.

Step Six: Associate pleasant feelings with free from cigarette smoking.

Step Seven: Use meditation or relaxation techniques with deep breathing and positive visualization.

Step Eight: Stay away from individuals or friends who smoke cigarettes.

Step Nine: Make physical exercise such as walking, jogging, bicycling, dancing, swimming, or weight lifting a part of your daily routine.

The purpose of the first five steps is to help you **develop a strong negative belief associated with pain** regarding smoking cigarettes (that you want to quit) and a positive belief associated with pleasure about refraining from it. The last four steps are designed to support you in achieving your goal.

Say the following to yourself:

- "I do not have to smoke cigarettes."
- "The negative outcome of cigarette smoking outweighs the positive outcome."
- "Smoking cigarettes is harmful to me and to my loved ones."
- "I can survive without smoking cigarettes."
- "I do not need it."

These affirmations will assist you on your path. You must repeat this process as often as you can until you develop a strong negative belief towards the cigarette smoking and stop using it. If you cannot stop your counterproductive addiction by yourself, consider help from Nicotine replacement treatment, Non-nicotine treatment, or Behavioral therapy professionals. However, the most critical element of your recovery comes from your wholehearted belief that smoking cigarettes that you are addicted to is severely harmful to you and your loved ones.

Steps to Overcoming Addiction to Substances

Taking the following steps will help you quit a substance to which you are addicted, such as coffee, tobacco, alcohol, food, or drugs.

Step One: Take a neutral stance about the substances that you are using by asking yourself these questions: "Do I have to use it?" "Can I survive without it?" "Can I get others' opinions about whether I should use it?"

Step Two: Make three separate lists of the positive, negative, and neutral consequences of using.

Step Three: Keep the list of the negative consequences of using substances on an index card and carry it with you.

Step Four: Read the negative consequences to yourself as often as possible, especially when you feel tempted by that substance.

Step Five: Associate that substance with the pain or negative consequences you have already experienced.

Step Six: Associate pleasant feelings with remaining substance free.

Step Seven: Use meditation or relaxation techniques with deep breathing and positive visualization.

Step Eight: Stay away from individuals or friends who abuse the substance in question.

Step Nine: Make physical exercise such as walking, jogging, bicycling, dancing, swimming, or weight lifting a part of your daily routine.

The purpose of the first five steps is to help you **develop a strong negative belief associated with pain** regarding the substance that you want to quit and a positive belief about abstaining from the substance. The last four steps are designed to support you in achieving your goal.

Say the following to yourself:

- "I do not have to use the substance."
- "The negative outcome of substance usage outweighs the positive outcome."
- "Using this substance is harmful to me and to my loved ones."

- "I can survive without it."
- "I do not need it!"

These affirmations will assist you on your path. You must repeat this process as often as you can until you develop a strong negative belief towards the substance and stop using it.

These methods can be used with any other habits or addictions that you have chosen to quit, such as domestic violence, overeating, using obscene language, making sarcastic remarks, promising without intention, displaying disrespectful behavior, arriving late to appointments, etc.

If you cannot stop your negative addiction by yourself, consider getting help from substance abuse counselors, rehabilitation centers, or hospitals. However, the most critical element of your recovery comes from your wholehearted belief that the substance that you are addicted to is severely harmful to you and your loved ones.

Steps to Overcoming Overeating

Many Americans overeat, a habit that often results in becoming obese. There are other societies that do not have this problem. Some societies view people who are overweight or obese as being well fed and rich. They are considered physically strong and influential. In addition, skinny or lean individuals may be overpowered by an overweight or obese person in a wrestling match.

Overeating has three-dimensional effects that occur in different proportions.

Positive Dimension: Eating food is a pleasure. Overeating helps us to gain weight. It helps us to remain satisfied for a long period of time.

Negative Dimension: Overeating may make us feel sleepy or sluggish. It causes unnecessary weight gain. The extra weight may cause physical and psychological problems such as high blood pressure, diabetes, bladder and kidney problems, and poor self-image.

Neutral Dimension: Some people may overeat and gain weight, while others may not.

Your conscious consumption of any food can be stopped, but it becomes difficult when you eat subconsciously, habitually, or addictively. In order to break your subconscious eating behavior, you need to identify and isolate the foods you eat habitually or addictively. If overeating is still a problem, take the following steps:

Step One: Seek advice from a nutritionist or medical practitioner about your food intake. Find out what kinds of food you are eating that are causing you to be overweight. Identify and isolate the foods that are causing you to gain extra weight, particularly cheese, butter, fatty meat, fried food, sugar, and rice.

Step Two: Think neutral thoughts about the foods that you have been eating habitually or addictively by asking yourself: "What are the positive, negative, and neutral benefits or outcomes of my eating these foods." Make positive, negative, and neutral lists and review them often.

Step Three: Write on an index card all the negative consequences of overeating these foods. Carry this index card with you and read it as often as possible, especially when you feel tempted by that food.

Step Four: Associate overeating that specific food with pain or negative consequences.

Step Five: Associate eating less of that identified specific food with good health and well-being.

Step Six: Stay away from individuals or friends who overeat and do not support your goal.

Step Seven: Use meditation, relaxation techniques, deep breathing, and positive visualizations.

Step Eight: Schedule physical exercise for yourself such as walking, jogging, bicycling, dancing, swimming, or weight lifting.

The purpose of the first four steps is to help you **develop an understanding of the negative consequences associated with pain** resulting from overeating. The purpose of the last four steps is to support you in achieving your goal.

Say to yourself:

- "Though I love food, I do not need to overeat."
- "The negative consequences of overeating outweigh the positive consequences."
- "Overeating is harmful to my physical health does not help my appearance."

These affirmations will place you on the path of de-programming your subconscious behavior of overeating. If you are following a diet program, you must continue. Do not quit. Use these steps as additional resources to help you reach your goal.

Summary

Our positive habits are essential to our success, wealth, peace, joy, and happiness. We must remember that our positive habits can become counterproductive habits that cause suffering. If we learn when to form good habits, then stopping our bad habits will be easier and we will be able to find deep, satisfying pleasure.

Questions

1. What are habits and addictions?
2. How do we form habits and addictions?
3. How can we get out of a habit or an addiction?
4. What are the steps to overcome a habit or an addiction?

UNDERSTANDING YOUR ANGRY SPOUSE OR PARTNER

Imagine you are away from your partner and feeling good. Your thoughts are positive toward your companion and you are looking forward to spending time with him or her. Once together, you don't feel the same because your partner is unhappy with you. What has changed? It could be that he or she is angry. Beware, anger is contagious! If your companion is angry, try to remain calm and pay close attention to your loved one. He or she is going through some mental, emotional, and/or physical pain. Perhaps he or she feels ignored and deceived, has lost something that is dear or valuable. These feelings are not necessarily caused by your actions. Whatever the cause, he or she is wearing an anger shield to protect a vulnerable heart.

Many psychotherapists believe that anger is not a primary emotion but rather a secondary emotion generated by a perceived threat, frustration, or injury. The injury could be physical, emotional, or psychological. Some people who have difficulty controlling their anger and those who injure themselves or others in expressing their anger were not trusted by the significant people in their childhood and adolescence. They have been ignored, injured, trivialized, rejected, or abused and have not found constructive ways of working through their anger.

Many people don't want to admit their primary feelings. You might have heard Melissa Manchester's song that goes, "Don't cry out loud. Keep it inside. Hide your feelings." Your partner may not feel comfortable acknowledging how afraid, frustrated, or hurt he or she is, especially when those feelings may indicate weakness. Many individuals feel that if they are perceived as weak, they will be taken advantage of. So, in an attempt to protect their egos, they may exhibit a tough, angry exterior.

Your angry partner needs your understanding and compassion—not lectures, or advice, about how to solve the problem First listen and acknowledge and validate your partner's feelings and do so without judging or condemning.

Listening in this way can be challenging. Can you embrace your partner with love and understanding? If not, you may need to take "timeout" to avoid catching your partner's anger as you would a common cold.

Timeout

The term "timeout" is used to describe someone silently walking away from a heated argument to diffuse the tension. In contrast, people who display angry gestures use obscene language, or slam doors as they leave an argument are fanning the fire. A "timeout" is very effective when both people have agreed to use this technique when a conflict escalates.

You have probably noticed that the timeout technique is used in many sporting events as a retreat, a way of cooling down, or an opportunity to plan a new strategy. Timeout is an effective method in helping individuals calm down and think clearly. It can be used in any place, any time, and in any human interaction.

When do you take timeout? When your anger starts rising in your body and mind. You monitor your physical symptoms, such as raised voice volume, flushing, increased breathing, tightened muscles, shaking, clenched fists, and sweating. During the timeout, you should not drive a vehicle unless you have to. Do not drink alcohol or use any illicit drugs. Do not go to a bar or any place where illegal substances are served. The best way to address your physical symptoms is to notice your negative thoughts and then focus on neutral and positive thoughts.

Using this technique can save relationships and lives by preventing physical, emotional, and verbal abuse. Animals react to situations, but humans have the ability to think before they respond. A timeout is used in sports to reorganize and rest before resuming a game. **Taking a timeout means stopping whatever you are engaged in doing to re-think, plan new strategies about how to improve your performance or situation.** A timeout has three dimensions: positive, negative, and neutral in different proportion. They are described below:

1. **Positive dimension:** A timeout will help an angry person calm down and think clearly. It will help prevent domestic violence. The risk of being arrested by police and going to jail will be eliminated.

2. **Negative dimension:** The issue of conflicts will be dropped and may never be resolved. A timeout can be used as a weapon to punish a person, as a way to avoid conflicts, and as way to make someone feel abandoned.

3. **Neutral dimension:** If one partner does not agree or allow the other to take timeout, it is ineffective.

When we compare the three dimensions, we find more positive results of timeout than negative and neutral ones. The thing to remember is that timeout will work only when it is used properly. First explain the concept and purpose of timeout to your partner. You could say, "We are together because we love each other. When we are together, there may be a time when we argue and get angry at each other. We might end up hurting each other emotionally. Sometimes fights escalate and someone gets hurt. Taking a timeout is a good way to protect ourselves, our relationship. We could agree ahead of time that when you or I feel that our anger is escalating during a discussion or an argument, we will take a timeout. You or I would go to another room, take a walk around the block, or visit the neighborhood coffee shop for thirty minutes or so. We will return back when we no longer feel angry. Then, we will discuss the problem or postpone resolving it until later. A timeout is not walking away to avoid discussing important issues that need to be resolved. The purpose of timeout is to prevent not only physical violence but also verbal and emotional violence.

When we are angry, a timeout helps us calm down, but it does not solve any problems that need to be addressed. To do that people need to practice positive self-talk and negotiate. The next section, "Understanding Our Communication Styles," explains the fundamentals of successful negotiation.

Self-Talk

What is self-talk? Many people misunderstand and think that it is something only crazy people who do That is not true. We all talk to ourselves vocally or silently every day. Our self-talk is a prelude to our behavior. What we see and experience, we interpret and talk to ourselves about, and then we behave or act. For example, we come home from work expecting that dinner is ready. We are hungry and see that dinner is not ready. What goes on in our minds? We may think negative, neutral, or positive thoughts. We may also talk to ourselves negatively, neutrally, or positively, saying:

1. **Negative self-talk:** I am hungry and my partner does not care for me. He or she has been at home all the day watching television or talking on telephone. He or she does not love me; otherwise, he or she would have prepared dinner for me.

2. **Neutral self-talk:** There must be some circumstantial reason that dinner is not ready. He or she may not be feeling well, or he or she has forgotten the time. Sometimes, it happens. It is not a big deal.

3. **Positive self-talk:** The world is uncertain. Even at restaurants, we have to wait to eat. This means I can have whatever I want for dinner. I will make a really great meal for two, and if he or she does not want any, then there's more for me.

The more we think and talk negatively, the more adrenalin and cortisol is produced in our bodies, which fuels our anger and can lead to violence. Prolonged negative thinking and negative self-talk may cause anxiety and depression. If we talk neutrally to ourselves, our bodies produce endorphins, and we feel calm and relaxed. It has been observed that people with anger problems are able to calm down and regain self-control by using the neutral and positive self-talk. When we start feeling angry, taking a timeout to read the following statements to ourselves can be helpful.

1. My anger is a signal to take a timeout and talk to myself.
2. I don't need to prove that I am right.
3. People are going to behave the way they want to, not the way I want them to.
4. It is easier to control myself than to control other people and situations.
5. If other people criticize me, there may be some truth in it.
6. I feel angry because things are not going my way.
7. I am angry because I am thinking negatively.
8. I need to relax and think neutrally or positively.
9. I might not have all the information.
10. I must obtain information from positive, negative, and neutral dimensions before I do anything.

Who Is Responsible for Our Anger?

Anger is an emotion that we experience from our infancy to old age. When we were children and misbehaved, our parents disciplined us, and we became unhappy or angry. When they bought us toys and candy or gave us hugs and kisses, we became happy. It is easy to conclude that other people make us happy, unhappy, or angry. We get angry when people are not nice to us and hold them responsible for our feelings and behaviors. If we become violent, we may even try to justify our violence, saying, "If you would not have insulted me, I would not have hit you." Or, "You broke your promise, so you're responsible for my anger and violent behavior." This kind of reasoning is a cognitive illusion. In much the same way, it appears to us that the sun is revolving around the Earth, but the opposite is true. It may appear that others cause our responses; however, we actually feel happy, unhappy, or angry according to the way we perceive, think, and interpret an event, object, or person. **We are responsible for our feelings and behavior.**

Affirmations to Stop Domestic Violence

1. I have the power of free will to choose.
2. It is my choice to be calm and gentle, or **furious, enraged, or violent**.
3. No one can make me **furious, enraged, or violent** unless I choose to be.
4. No one is responsible for my violent behavior except me.
5. Getting furious, enraged, or violent is harmful to me and to my loved ones.
6. It is necessary for me to remain calm and positive to enjoy my loved ones.
7. When I choose to be with my loved ones, I will respect their likes, dislikes, ideas, and feelings, even though they may be completely different than mine.
8. I will not use force to control or teach my loved ones, even though I think that my ideas and values may be beneficial to them. I will teach them with empathy, patience, and love.

Summary

We live together to enjoy each other's company, giving love and support to one another. The differences in our family backgrounds, tastes, values, and levels of education differ—sometimes make it difficult to get along. If we learn to cooperate, respect, and love one another, our relationships can be a heavenly experience on earth

Questions

1. What is a timeout?
2. What is self-talk?
3. Who is responsible for our anger?

Exercise

Your relationship with Your Partner

1. Negative Dimension: Write down all of your negative feelings.
2. Neutral Dimension: Write down all your neutral feelings.
3. Positive Dimension: Write down all your positive feelings.
4. 4. Evaluation: In which dimension the highest percent or degree of good or benefit is for you?

UNDERSTANDING OUR COMMUNICATION STYLES

Today appears to be the communication age. You see people talking on cell phones while they are walking on the street and driving cars on the road. There was a time when people communicated by mail, and this would take weeks or months to arrive. Today, the speed of communication has increased exponentially. Communication is the lifeline of families, friendships, and organizations. We communicate with words, gestures, body language, tone of voice, and facial expressions. The words we say, how we say them, and when we say them have different meanings to different people.

There was a time when families built their own homes and produced their own food and clothes. Today, we live in an advanced industrial society in which we are all interdependent on each other for our growth and survival. Anything we need to sustain our lives comes from other people—not only food, clothes, money and housing but also love, respect, and recognition. To thrive we must learn to communicate effectively with our fellow human beings, especially those closest to us.

Who is responsible for communication? It takes two people or two parties to communicate as speaker and listener. The speaker needs active cooperation and willingness from the listener during the communication process. The listener is not obligated to listen to the speaker. It is the speaker's responsibility to use words, gestures, body language, tone of voice, and facial expressions to gain interest from the listener. The effectiveness of the listener's participation in communication depends on the listener's previous listening experience, education, family background, and present emotional state. The success of communication depends on the listener's capability to interpret the speaker's intended meaning. When the listener does not interpret the speaker's message accurately, the communication has failed. When we are unaware of the essential ingredients of the dynamics between a speaker and a listener, we can fail as leaders, employees, and partners.

Generally, the majority of us have no problem communicating with our co-workers and partners when we both (speaker and listener) are calm. However, if one of us is hurt, angry, or unhappy, difficulties often arise. When we are furious or enraged, our communication system breaks down, as does our logical thinking. During this time, our minds do not function at an optimum level and our communication skills are compromised. In order to restore our communication skills, we must change our negative thoughts to neutral and/or positive thoughts. Our neutral thoughts produce neutral feelings by ceasing the secretion of chemicals in our bodies—which helps us to calm down from anxiety or anger—and propel us to speak in a neutral communication style. Our positive thoughts produce positive feelings by generating positive chemicals such as endorphins in our bodies, which enable us to speak in a positive communication style. As you can see, our emotional state has a powerful influence on our communication styles. However, we have the power to choose our feelings by choosing our thoughts and expressing them appropriately.

Four Styles of Communication

There are four styles of communication we use in our day-to-day lives. They are positive, negative, neutral, and a mixture of the three. The components of these communication styles are described below.

1. **Positive communication style** is the expression of positive thoughts, feelings, words, gestures, body language, tone of voice, and facial expressions. This communication style is especially effective and powerful for partners in an intimate relationship. The positive thinking and feeling are such powerful ingredients in communicating that people fall in love with each other without speaking the same language.

2. **Negative communication style** is the expression of negative thoughts, feelings, words, gestures, body language, tone of voice, and facial expressions. This communication style is especially effective when persuasion is called for—as in saying no to a car dealer who is pulling out all the stops to get you to sign a sales agreement.

3. **Neutral communication style** is the expression of neutral thoughts, feelings, words, gestures, body language, tone of voice, and facial expressions. This communication style is very effective in relating to strangers.

4. **Mixed communication style** is the expression of mixed thoughts and/or feelings that include any combination of positive, negative, or neutral words, gestures, body language, tone of voice, and or facial expressions. Keep in mind that the mixed communication style has various combinations of expression. This communication style is very effective in a comedy performance.

When communication breaks down it may be difficult to pinpoint where we went wrong. We assume the listener is thinking and feeling the way we do. We may have no empathy and patience for the listener. We ignore the fact that factors such as our education, training, personalities affect how we perceive the world, how we interpret what someone says. We ignore the right of the listener to think, feel, and interpret differently than we do. We expect the listener to read our minds and understand hints and cues. Many of us present our thoughts and feelings in a mixed communication style with conflicting messages and ideas. For example, if an angry man shouts, "I love you" at his wife the words, she hears positive words spoken in a derisive tone. The contrast is likely to confuse and maybe even frighten her.

Couples hurt one another emotionally for petty reasons, thinking that it will be forgotten or will go away the next day. Unfortunately, unresolved feelings do not go away; they accumulate over a period of time. Every time a person is hurt, he or she loses a degree of respect, trust, and love for his or her offender. Verbal fights break out between couples when they are tired of suffering from accumulated hurt feelings and as a result have difficulty communicating with each other.

Restoring Communication between Spouses or Partners

In order to restore communication between you and your partner, you must remove the roadblocks. You must settle the differences and resolve the past hurt feelings. You must overcome your anger and fear through neutral thinking. Refrain from using the negative and mixed communication styles. Remember that you cannot gain respect, love, and cooperation by threatening, condemning, or criticizing your loved ones. Use the positive communication style when you are speaking to your partner.

Here are three ways to resolve hurt feelings: (a) acknowledge the hurtful things you have said with an apology, (b) pay restitution for the emotional damage, and (c) request forgiveness.

Behaving positively towards the offended individual is vital in helping them resolving hurt feelings. If a simple apology does not satisfy the offended person, you might think about paying restitution.

Restitution is a compensation rendered to the hurt person. It may be giving flowers, doing a favor, or a monetary payment. but also it may be providing goods and services. The offender acknowledges his or her wrongdoing and initiates a negotiation while admitting and accepting the consequences by paying the compensation for the emotional damage done to his or her partner.

There are some emotional damages that cannot be repaired by a simple apology or with compensation. The offender may request forgiveness and the offended person may choose to forgive him or her. When the offended person forgives the offender, the communication line between them will be restored and normalized. However, the offended partner may still have some negative feelings of fear, hurt, or frustration. These feelings need to be discussed and negotiated at a time when both of you are calm. When you communicate with each other, **you must use a positive communication style,** showing understanding, empathy, love, and compassion in order to restore intimacy and maintain a loving relationship.

Summary

Communication skills are essential for creating our success, wealth, peace, joy, and happiness. In this modern society, nearly everything we need to sustain our lives comes from other people, including food, clothes, as well as love, respect, recognition, prestige and fame. If we want to thrive, we must learn skills to communicate effectively with others.

Questions

1. What is your communication style?
2. What are the roadblocks to effective communication?
3. Why a leader does fail to communicate with his supporters?

4. Why a sales person does fail to communicate with his customers?

5. Why does a partner fail to communicate with their loved ones?

6. How can we restore broken communication?

UNDERSTANDING CONFLICTS WITH YOUR SPOUSE OR PARTNER

You and your partner are together because you love each other and have developed a deep intimacy between you. However, when a conflict arises between you, you may perceive it as a threat to your relationship. You may question whether or not your affection is genuine. You may start fighting—verbally and physically—or even talking about breaking up.

Conflicts are natural and inevitable in human relationships because we are dynamic, not static. At times we are selfish and do things only to please ourselves; while at other times another person's needs take first priority.

Three Dimensions of Conflict

Conflict has three dimensions: positive, negative, and neutral.

Positive Dimension: Conflict provides an opportunity to upgrade or downgrade relationships. When conflict is resolved, mutual trust and mutual respect are increased. Both parties may be bonded and may experience higher satisfaction and the relationship becomes better than before.

Negative Dimension: Conflict can promote selfishness and create enemies, and foster unfair treatment such as verbal or physical abuse. It promotes blaming, fault-finding, arguing, and violence.

Neutral Dimension: Conflict can be neutralized and resolved by talking about mutual interests, benefits, well-being, and losses. When we perceive the neutral dimension, we shrug our shoulders and say, "Whatever will be, will be." There is no blaming or complaining about the conflict or situation.

Since conflicts are inevitable, we must learn to resolve them positively and peacefully. Couples who are able to handle conflict in a positive manner maintain good mental health and have better relationships, deeper intimacy, and stronger bonding than those who struggle with ongoing frustration, anger, fights, and violence. Here are some examples of common conflicts most couples encounter:

- You and your partner have one car but each of you wants to go to a different place.

- You and your partner have one TV and each of you wants to watch a different show.

- It's dinnertime and you have decided you'll dine out. You want to eat at Marie Calendar's and your partner wants to eat at Red Lobster.

- The house is a mess. You think it's your partner's turn; he or she thinks its yours.

- You want your partner to pay the bills, but he or she wants you to pay them.

Make a list of some recent conflicts between you and your partner. Were they resolved in a peaceful way, or are you still frustrated, angry, or resentful about the outcome? We have the freedom to focus on the positive, negative, or neutral dimensions of an object, person, or situation and will think, feel, and behave accordingly.

Let us go back and resolve one of the above examples of common conflicts by utilizing three-dimensional strategies.

CONFLICT: A couple has only one car and each person wishes to go to a different place.

Positive Conflict Resolution: By focusing on the positive dimension of the conflict, we choose to resolve it positively and peacefully. In this scenario, both partners try to resolve the conflict by coming up with solutions that may include but are not limited to:

1. Creating a schedule at the beginning of the week that gives each turns with the car at agreed upon times
2. Driving together
3. Carpooling
4. Keeping communication lines open throughout the day by discussing ahead of time the needs each person has for using the car
5. Creating a team effort by collaborating with each other regarding any last-minute changes
6. Respecting each other's feelings and needs

Negative Conflict Resolution: By focusing on the negative dimension of the conflict, we choose to resolve it with anger, intimidation, or violence. Here, one or both partners think negatively towards the conflict and attempt to resolve it in a selfish manner. The angry partner may demand the car and may not care about the other person's feelings. The angry partner feels justified in using the car. The other partner experiences stress and perceives him or her as the enemy. Also, both partners may internalize the anger from the argument and see each other as selfish. Both partners may feel that they are being treated unfairly by the other. Their verbal fighting and argument may escalate to domestic violence.

Neutral Conflict Resolution: When we focus on the neutral dimension of the conflict, we choose to resolve it "as-is." It does not matter who gets to drive the car. Neither partner minds changing his/her schedule. Or one partner lets the other take the car and finds some other solution, such as asking a friend or neighbor for a ride. He or she may decide to take the bus or a taxi to reach his or her destination.

Summary

We must remember that conflict is part of our lives. If we choose to resolve a conflict by focusing on the positive or neutral dimensions, chances are we will experience little or no difficulties in resolving conflicts. But if one or both people in a partnership choose to focus on the negative dimension, resolving the conflict will be difficult. If one of us or both of us is thinking negatively, then we need to take a "timeout" to remain calm. At a later time, we will both be able to resolve the conflict with positive thinking.

Questions

1. What is conflict?
2. What are the three dimensions of conflict?
3. What are the best ways to resolve conflicts?

UNDERSTANDING OUR PROBLEMS

Three Dimensions of the Problem

Every day we talk about problems in our neighborhood, nation, and world. Problems such as hunger, disease, wars, terrorism, government corruption, and rising gasoline prices are part of our daily conversations. At home, we may have problems paying our bills, managing our diabetes, keeping rats out of our basement.

Each problem has three possible dimensions: positive, negative, and neutral.

Positive Dimension: The problem demands our attention to improve things or situations so we can enjoy our lives. Problems generate work for us. If other people do not have problems, we do not have jobs.

Negative Dimension: The problem can be a threat to our existence or well-being. It may cost us money and time. It may be painful and cause suffering.

Neutral Dimension: What may be a problem to one person is a "piece of cake" to another. A problem for some creates jobs for others.

What Is a Problem? Is it Something We Don't Like?

In order to solve a problem, we must be able to identify it. A problem is determined by our perceptions, interpretations, and beliefs about a thing, person, or situation. To a homeowner, a leaky pipe can be a problem, but to a plumber it is an opportunity to earn money. To a schoolboy who dislikes school, going to school can be a problem, but to the schoolteacher, it is a meaningful profession. For someone who uses a wheelchair, a snowstorm can be a problem. To an avid skier, snow is a dream come true.

The common cause of a problem is that we do not like something. So, once the thing, person, or situation that we do not like is brought to our attention, it can be resolved. In order to resolve it, we need to focus on the neutral dimension and step back from the identified problem to gather information from all three-dimensional. Doing so will help us act in a responsible, helpful way.

If we think that the problem is significant and we do not resolve it, we continue stewing about it. Our bodies and minds will experience distress until we resolve it.

Who Is Right and Who Is Wrong?

"Birds a feather flock together."

"Opposites attract."

The above well-known sayings demonstrate two opposing ideas. In some cases, those with similar thinking tend to "flock together" in solidarity. Other times people who are different from one another are drawn to together. But no matter who we surround ourselves with, we will come across people whose views are different from our own.

Couples, families, organizations and nations fight to prove that they are right and that others are wrong. While our own values are dear to us, they will clash with the values of others. One conclusion we often draw is that one set of values is right and the other wrong. However, individuals, groups, organizations, or nations who are fighting with each other can be right from their own perspectives.

Imagine a family situation. The wife says that she wants her husband to spend time with her and their children. Her husband says that he is too busy at work earning enough money to provide for the family. Now the question arises who is right and who is wrong? Who cares more about the family? The answer is that both are right; they both care. The wife is concerned for the emotional well-being of the family while the husband is focused on the financial well-being of the family.

What can you do to solve the problem when both are right? There are three strategies: negotiate, take a timeout, and accept. You may use one of these three strategies by applying three-dimensional thinking. In this case, the best strategy is to negotiate. Both the wife and husband need to find a neutral ground (neutral dimension) where both of them can freely discuss their common interests and what the family gains and loses with either of their plans. If they do, they will be able to find a common ground and balance their two concerns.

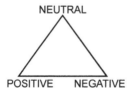

Absolute Thinking: All or Nothing

Many couples who seek marriage counseling say that they have communication problems and difficulty relating with trusting each other. They complain that their partners are not the same people that they used to be. They do not feel the same love, respect, and romance that they felt at the time of their marriage.

Most couples get married because they love, respect, trust, and communicate well with each other; otherwise, they would not have gotten married. What happens to these couples as time passes by? They both change and inevitably the relationship does as well.

From the moment we are born, we grow and change every day. Our lives are not static but dynamic. We are constantly expanding and evolving. Sometimes, we don't recognize that we are changing, but our photographs prove that we have. What we were yesterday, we are not today. When a spouse or partner is unaware of his or her own constant change and wants or expects the other spouse or partner not to change, he or she may experience tension, anger, loss of love, and communication difficulties. Expecting our partners to be the same as when we first met them will only disappoint us.

We search for happiness, and when we find it, we love to hold on to it. When it disappears, we wonder whether it was an illusion. The happiness was real, but not permanent. We see a beautiful sunset that lasts only for half an hour. Feelings of joy, like the sunset, are not static. They fluctuate in degree and intensity—every hour, every minute. When we try to hold fast on to our happiness,, we are disappointed because we are asking for something that cannot be. We must acknowledge and learn to enjoy the moment and let it go with our good wishes. Then let us give and receive the new joy and happiness.

Why do many people not know how to enjoy the present moment? Perhaps it is due to a lack of attention or awareness. Sometimes, it may be just worries about the future or past. Suppose that a university student is failing his classes. He is not paying attention to the lectures or doing his homework. Instead, he is daydreaming about seeing his girlfriend. After class, he keeps talking to his girlfriend about his frustration of not doing well in class and being unable to relax or enjoy her company. He cannot concentrate on his schoolwork because he is thinking about his girlfriend and cannot enjoy his girlfriend because he is concerned about failing his classes. His girlfriend expected to have fun and enjoyment with him instead of him being boring and worrisome. She became tired of his behavior and one day told him that she wanted to break up with him, he became angry and violent with her. His neighbor called the police, who arrested him and took him to jail. After two days in jail, he was taken to the court. The judge gave him two choices. He could take this case to a jury trial, pleading not guilty, or he could stay on summary probation for three years and complete a year-long weekly domestic violence intervention program. He decided to enroll in the program. He learned to control his anger and not resort to violence. He learned to pay attention and enjoy the positive moments and take a "timeout" from the negative moments. He completed the program with distinction.

Forgiveness

"Making mistakes is human, forgiving is divine," wrote Spencer W. Kimball, the author of *The Miracle of Forgiveness*. Kimball explained that forgiving is so powerful that it brings peace to the tormented soul. We must forgive so that our desire for revenge does not erode our emotional well-being. In fact, clinical findings suggest that forgiveness helps prevent anxiety, depression, and many other psychological disorders.

When you forgive, you are not doing any favor to your offender unless he or she owes you money or something. **You are forgiving your offender mainly to do a favor to yourself.** Your pain and other disturbing feelings will go away when you forgive. If you hold a grudge against your offender, your body and mind will retain those feelings and suffer as a result. By forgiving, you help your body and mind to heal.

When you forgive, it does not mean that you are approving of your offender's wrongful behavior or allowing domestic violence to continue in the future. We must respond to the present and future wrongful behavior or domestic violence with appropriate strategies. In a domestic violence incident, we must take a **timeout**, which can include obtaining a restraining order, which can be followed by negotiating with the perpetrator to prevent wrongful behavior or domestic violence in the future. The third choice is being indifferent or unconcerned—not a safe option given the dangers involved. Whatever choice you make, remember that your love alone is not enough to solve all relationships issues; both people must learn skills and strategies to maintain and keep a relationship healthy.

CHAPTER FOUR

UNDERSTANDING DOMESTIC VIOLENCE

(**A note to the reader:** Domestic violence as explained here is applicable in Orange County and Los Angeles County, California. It may differ in other counties and states. Therefore, it is suggested that you contact your local law library for current information that applies to where you live.)

According to *Webster's Seventh New Collegiate Dictionary*, violence is "exertion of physical force so as to injure or abuse, an instance of violent treatment or procedure, injury by or as if by distortion, infringement, or profanation; intense turbulent or furious often destructive action or force."

Violence is viewed by our society as an act of homicide, assault, or domestic violence. Domestic violence consists of spousal or partner abuse, child abuse, and elder abuse. Child abuse and elder abuse are not discussed in this book.

The term violence is misunderstood by many people, especially by the perpetrators of domestic violence. They tend to identify violence as only murder and serious physical assault. However, violence also consists of pushing, shoving, grabbing, slapping, intimidating, name-calling, physical or emotional threats, and sex without consent of the partner. Perpetrators who don't consider these actions as domestic violence, become surprised and angry when they are arrested and punished for their actions. Therefore, it is very important to understand the nature of violence and what constitutes it.

People can be arrested and sentenced for using force, threats, and intimidation to control a partner. Pushing, shoving, grabbing, or holding when both you and your mate are in a happy mood does not constitute a crime and is not punishable by the law. Only when the physical contact is unwanted is considered a crime that is punishable with a fine and imprisonment.

Three Dimensions of Violence

Violence has three dimensions: positive, negative, and neutral.

Positive Dimension: Violence may be used as self-defense by an individual, group, or nation. It may be justified as a way to protect yourself your loved ones or your nation. It may help enforce control over a situation temporarily.

Negative Dimension: Violence is against the law. Usually, instead of controlling a problem, violence escalates it. For a time you may be able to wield control through violence, but you could very well suffer at the hands of another's violence toward you. And if caught, you may have to pay restitution and penalty and possibly go to jail. During a violent incident, your actions may even cost the loss of another's life or your own.

Neutral Dimension: Violence does not guarantee you a positive or negative outcome. The neutral dimension—as with the positive dimension—helps individuals, groups, and nations release emotional tension. It provides options such as negotiation, timeout, and acceptance to find long lasting solutions.

If you would like to check the positive outcomes of the use of violence, place the positive, negative, and neutral dimensional effects in the angles of the triangle below.

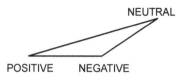

You will notice that the negative angle is larger than the positive and neutral angles, which means there are more negative outcomes than positive or neutral ones; we can conclude that the use of violence is not an effective method for resolving conflicts.

What Is Domestic Violence?

Domestic violence is misunderstood by many people. Some think that it is a private family matter that occurs among uneducated minorities. Some believe that it happens only between mentally ill couples. On the contrary, it occurs with people of all races, ethnicities, and religions as well as social and economic backgrounds. It is as serious a problem as drug and alcohol abuse. It is not limited to couples that live together but also includes children, the elderly, and individuals in dating relationships. The batterers come from all professional backgrounds, including doctors, law enforcement officers, educators, and ministers.

A domestically violent person tries to use force to bend family members to his or her will. The batterer deliberately inflicts physical or emotional pain to the victim to keep the victim under his or her control. Domestic violence is no longer just a private family matter; it is a serious crime punishable by fine and imprisonment.

The term "domestic violence" represents a big umbrella that covers many legal and criminal issues related to family members and friends. The legal definition of domestic violence as defined by California Penal Code Section 13700 is as follows:

> "Abuse" means intentionally or recklessly causing or attempting to cause bodily injury, or placing another person in reasonable apprehension of imminent serious bodily injury to himself or herself, or another. "Domestic violence" means abuse committed against an adult or a fully emancipated minor who

is a spouse, former spouse, cohabitant, former cohabitant, or person with whom the suspect has a child or is having or has had a dating or engagement relationship.

For purposes of this subdivision, "cohabitant" means two unrelated adult persons living together for a substantial period of time, resulting in some permanency or relationship. Factors that may determine whether persons are cohabitating include, but are not limited to: (1) sexual relations between parties, while sharing the same living quarters, (2) sharing of income or expenses, (3) joint use or ownership of property, (4) whether the parties hold themselves out as husband and wife, (5) continuity of the relationship, and (6) the length of the relationship.

The term "abuse" as defined under Penal Code 13700 has two distinct parts: The first, "intentionally or recklessly causing or attempting to cause bodily injury," which refers to actual batteries. The second part deals with "placing another person in reasonable apprehension of imminent, serious bodily injury to himself or another." This refers to threats made by the suspect and fear perceived by the victim.

The general definition of domestic violence includes but is not limited to physical, verbal, emotional, sexual, or economic abuse.

Physical Abuse: The following methods are used by the batterer to intimidate and control the victim.

- Threatening to hurt or kill the victim
- Intimidating the victim by raising a fist
- Forcing the victim to do something against his or her will
- Restraining the victim from moving or leaving
- Pointing a finger as a gun
- Waving a knife
- Pulling a victim's clothing, hair, arms, or legs
- Throwing food or drinks at the victim
- Pushing or shoving

- Grabbing or pinching
- Sitting on or pinning the victim
- Biting or spitting
- Kicking or stomping
- Slapping or punching
- Hitting with a belt or any other object
- Choking or holding a hand over the victim's mouth
- Destroying property or hurting pets

Verbal Abuse: Verbal abuse consists of words, phrases, or terms that are spoken or written with the intent to hurt, scare, intimidate, threaten, demean, or belittle the victim. Such abuse includes but is not limited to voice volume, tone, and body language to control the victim. Verbal abuse is the prelude of physical abuse. Usually physical abuse starts after verbal abuse. Verbal abuse also includes

- Screaming or yelling during a conversation
- Swearing or insulting
- Name-calling or humiliating
- Using obscene language
- Leaving insulting messages on the telephone answering machine
- Using labels such as stupid, idiot, or scatterbrain
- Threatening to harm the victim in any other way

Emotional Abuse: Emotional abuse consists of creating a climate of control through fear and intimidation. One example may be making threatening statements such as: "If you do this you will never see your children again, or you will never see your parents again." Another form is claiming entitlement of superior status and treating the partner as a servant or trash. A batterer often induces fear and guilt, thus obtaining compliance to his or her demand from the victim. The batterer makes all major decisions for the household without consulting the partner. This is a deliberate attack to the victim's self-esteem and self-worth. Emotional abuse includes but is not limited to

- Telling the victim that he or she is mentally sick or crazy
- Deliberately causing anxiety or depression to control the victim
- Inducing guilt
- Telling lies and providing false information
- Threatening to gain custody of the children by proving the victim an incompetent parent
- Threatening to kill the victim's relatives and parents
- Name-calling, e.g., dumb, ugly, fat, couch potato, lazy, unfit parent, or trash
- Degrading, embarrassing, or humiliating
- Belittling in front of family and friends
- Forbidding the victim to make new friends or have contact with old friends
- Ban visiting or communicating with relatives
- Constantly monitoring whereabouts of the victim

Sexual Abuse: Sexual abuse consists of having sex with the partner by use of physical force, threats, intimidation, manipulation, or putting pressure on the person to perform any sexual act against one's will. Sex is defined as any contact with any part of another's body that is considered by the victim to be a sexual organ or sexually erotic part of the body. The purpose of the batterer who abuses sexually is to display power and authority to control, humiliate, and subjugate the victim. Sexual abuse includes but is not limited to

- Rape, forcing sex
- Forcing sex while the partner is asleep
- Withholding sex
- Forcing a partner to view pornography
- Forcing unwanted sexual contact

- Assaulting breasts or genitals
- Keeping secret a personal sexually transmitted disease
- Forcing the partner to have sex with others
- Coercing into prostitution
- Engaging in a violent sex act

Economic Abuse: Economic abuse consists of controlling or restricting a partner to access of money by hiding assets and bank accounts, depriving access to financial resources, or letting the partner suffer without food or daily necessities. Economic abuse includes but is not limited to

- Forcing the victim to give his or her paycheck and not allowing him or her to spend any of it
- Withholding funds and giving allowance to the victim if asked
- Making the victim beg for money
- Forcing the victim to stay home
- Discouraging the victim from seeking gainful employment
- Keeping the victim totally dependent on the batterer

Is Domestic Violence a Joke?

What is socially accepted in movies and TV (a slap in the face to a man) is very different from reality. Here are two stories of "real-life" incidents that may occur both on television and in real-life, but in real life there are serious consequences.

Story No. 1

Rachelle is a fifty-four-year-old grandmother. She is gainfully employed as a business executive in Orange County. She has one daughter, Christina. Rachelle and Christina get along very well together and have never had any major problems with each other. Christina is married to Alex. Christina and Alex have been married for five years and have a son named Paul, who is four years old. Alex and Christina argue and verbally fight occasionally about disciplining Paul.

Rachelle lives alone in Orange County, and Christina's family reside in Riverside County. That is about a two-hour drive for Rachelle. She doesn't mind. She loves to play with Paul and walk with him around the neighborhood. Paul loves her too because of the special attention and generous gifts she gives him.

Christina and Alex invited Rachelle for a Sunday lunch. Rachelle gladly accepted the invitation. Traffic was good, and her spirits were high. She arrived around 11 a.m. Lunch went well. They had planned to go to the mall after lunch. They were getting into a minivan and Christina had a problem with Paul. Frustrate, Paul started having a temper tantrum. Alex did not understand what the problem was. He glanced over his shoulder and noticed that Paul was putting up a good battle with Christina. Alex got out of the car and walked around angrily to where Christina was struggling with Paul to place him into his car seat. Alex told Christina what an incompetent mother she was and that she needed to show Paul who was in charge. Rachelle, without saying a word, reached Alex and slapped his face to let him know that she was in charge. Alex drove to the mall and nobody spoke anymore about the incident. Rachelle returned back to her home in Orange County that evening.

About two weeks later, Rachelle received a notice to appear at the Riverside Court. It turned out that Alex filed a report against Rachelle on assault and battery charges. She was surprised and thought that it was a joke. Rachelle had to appear in front of a judge, which was not a joke. She admitted to slapping Alex and explained the situation to the judge. The judge gave her two choices. She can either take this case to a jury trial insisting she did nothing wrong or she can stay on summary probation for three years and complete a year-long weekly domestic violence intervention program. Rachelle decided to attend the domestic violence intervention program.

Story No. 2

John and Mary have been married for four years. John has an eleven-year-old daughter, Michelle, from his previous marriage. Mary has a fourteen-year-old son, David, from her previous marriage. They have one daughter together, Christi, who is three years old. John was working for the aerospace industry but had been laid off from work because of a budget cut. Mary was working as a checker at a Super K-mart. She often came home tired and had no energy to do any housework. John and Mary frequently fought over house chores or bill payments. On Mary's birthday, John, Michelle, and David planned a party for her. Everyone bought a birthday gift for Mary. Mary hated to eat spinach. As a joke, John brought frozen packaged spinach, wrapped it nicely, and gave it to Mary as a birthday present. Mary was excited and opened the gift only to find it was spinach. She became furious and picked up the birthday cake cutting knife in one hand and grabbed John's shirt collars with the other hand shouting, "How dare you do this to me?" Michelle got scared and dialed 911 for help. Within ten minutes the police were there to investigate. They interviewed each family member individually. John had fingernail scratches on his neck. The police announced that she was under arrest for domestic violence. She spent two days in jail and was released on a plea bargain that she would stay on summary probation for three years and complete a year-long weekly domestic violence intervention program.

Is Domestic Violence a Nightmare?

Here is a true story from one of our clients who has changed her name for confidentiality"

"My name is Kathy and I am twenty-eight years old. I live by myself and work for an international corporation as a unit supervisor. I have a lot of responsibility on my shoulders, but I like it. I have a loving and adorable grandmother who is in her eighties. She told me that my uncle lost his job because of his drug and alcohol problems. He has been in and out of jobs and can't support his wife. Finally, his wife kicked him out and he had no place to go, so my grandmother let him move in with her. She asked if I could visit them one weekend.

"I drove to her house on a Saturday morning. Her living room was a total mess—dirty clothes mixed with clean clothes on the floor, cigarette butts strewn about, and the place smelled with a nasty odor. I called Grandma outside. I asked her if my uncle was doing drugs in the house. Before I knew it, my uncle came outside and began to argue with me, in front of Grandma. Apparently, he had overheard our conversation. He started accusing me and pointing his finger in my face; I don't know what he was saying. All I remember is a strong smell coming out of his mouth. I turned around and headed back through the kitchen door. He followed me closely. Once inside the kitchen, he picked up a chair and started to attack me, pushing the chair into my back and forcing me out of the house. I felt a lot of pain. I told him to stop. I told him that it was hurting me. He didn't listen. All I remember is turning around and grabbing a kitchen knife; I thought that I had to protect myself from this person charging at me with a chair. The neighbors called the police, probably because we made a lot of noise. I was angry and screaming at him. I was wondering, *how did a knife end up in my hand*? Grandma was in tears. Though both my uncle and I lost control, I was the one who was placed under arrest and booked on assault with a deadly weapon.

"I spent three days in jail. It was the most terrifying three days in my life. I didn't sleep. I didn't eat. I still have nightmares of that experience. After seventy-two long hours of hell, I was ordered to sixty days of house arrest. In addition, I was ordered to complete a year-long weekly domestic violence intervention program."

Is Domestic Violence a Mistake?

A Story of a Medical Doctor

Michael and Shelley have been married for about fifteen years. They have one daughter Cindy, age 15, and two sons—Matt, age 12, and John, age 10. Michael is a medical doctor and owns an emergency medical clinic. Shelley is the office manager of the clinic with responsibilities of records keeping and managing the business and household finances. They bought a boat on a monthly installment payment plan. Michael, John, Matt, Cindy, and their friends loved to go boating on weekends. Shelley does not know how to swim and is afraid of deep water. She went a couple of times with them but then stopped going. After few months the boat manufacturing corporation repossessed the boat and took away from the marina because of failure to make monthly payments for three months. Shelley stopped making the payment because she did not like to stay at home alone while everyone else was having fun. One weekend Michael, Matt, John, Cindy, and their friends went to marina to get the boat only to find it gone. Michael found out that his boat has been repossessed by the seller and why. Michael returned back home and found Shelley watching TV in the living room. He was angry and slapped her couple of times. She wanted to get away from him and he grabbed her blouse. Her blouse torn apart and he let her go. She called 911 the police. The police arrived in fifteen minutes. Police interviewed Shelley and Michael separately. Shelley told the police about the incident and showed her torn blouse. The Police arrested Michael and took him to jail. It was Saturday and he could not be bailed out until Monday. On Monday he was released from the jail on three years' summary probation and completion of a year-long weekly domestic violence intervention program.

A Story of a City Mayor

Jim and Linda are high school sweet hearts have been married for twenty-six years. They have a daughter and a son, both of whom are married and live on their own. Jim is a highly respected mayor of the city where he and Linda live. Jim and Linda met a beautiful unmarried attorney, Melody, who was very supportive to Jim during his campaign. Jim and Melody would have lunch together and discuss politics. One evening Jim called Linda and told her that he is going to a town hall meeting with Melody and probably would be home late. Linda loved Jim wholeheartedly but became suspicious that Jim having an affair with Melody. Linda waited for Jim to come home for dinner, but he did not come back. She could not go to sleep. She stayed awake and waited to confront Jim. He returned home about 3:00 a.m. and was heading towards the bathroom. Linda blocked him and asked if he is having any affair with Melody. Jim got upset and pushed her away and went to the bathroom. Linda fell down and hurt her ankle. She got up and went to sleep. In the morning she discovered that her ankle was swollen and that it was painful to walk. She went to a medical clinic for treatment. The doctor inquired her how it happened. She told that she fell down when her husband pushed her away during an argument. The doctor explained that he was mandated by law to report the police about any domestic violence incident. Linda said that she loved her husband and did not want make any report. Even so, the doctor reported the incident to the police. The police arrested Jim and took him to police custody. Melody went to bail Jim out. The case was presented to the judge. The judge gave him two options. He could either take his case to a jury trial insisting he did nothing wrong or he can stay on summary probation for three years and complete a year-long weekly domestic violence intervention program. He decided to stay on probation and complete the program.

What Are the Causes of Domestic Violence?

There are misunderstandings about the causes of domestic violence. Some people blame the victim for causing the domestic violence. Some people believe that it is the batterer's inability to control his or her anger. However, most batterers' records show no prior incident of losing control in public places or on their jobs. The research shows that many batterers do not have a history of violence with others except their partners. Other people think that marital, financial, or substance abuse problems are the cause of domestic violence. These assumptions camouflage the main cause of the domestic violence.

The root cause of domestic violence is that the batterer is trying to dominate and gain control over the victim as well as maintain his or her own self-esteem and self-worth. When the victim defies or ignores the authority of the batterer, the batterer feels discounted and abandoned. He or she also feels a loss of power, authority, self-worth, and self-dignity. The batterer inflicts pain on the victim to restore his or her authority, self-dignity, and control over the victim. The batterer, not the source of the conflict, such as infidelity, is the cause of the violent behavior. Therefore the two problems need to be addressed separately. Our views of the world and beliefs determine our behavior. The directly contributing factor is the batterer's belief using force to control his or her partner is an appropriate way to behave. The following are some typical batterer's beliefs:

- It is okay to be violent to defend myself.
- It is okay to respond violently to provocation.
- I am superior to the victim.
- Both partners are responsible for domestic violence.
- My violence is justified when my partner starts it.
- A little pushing or slapping is not a violent behavior.
- During a heated argument, everybody uses name-calling such as bitch, whore, bastard, or son of a bitch.
- All couples fight physically once in awhile.
- I have the right to choose my partner's friends.
- I have the right to monitor the whereabouts of my partner.
- Jealousy is a sign of love.

Understanding the Domestic Violence Law

In order to understand the current domestic violence law, you must know about its origin and evolution. Back in the sixteenth century, British common law allowed husbands to beat their wives with a stick no thicker than their thumb, i.e., "the rule of thumb law." The courts not only allowed domestic violence to occur, they also provided guidelines informing husbands how to "correct" their wives.

The British common law is part of the legal tradition that formed a large part of modern English and American law. It was not until the Civil Rights and Women's Rights movements that laws in the United States were written prohibiting domestic violence. In an attempt to further understand the evolution of domestic violence in early America, it is significant to note that wealthy individuals "owned" slaves, indentured servants, and their wives. Females were merely considered men's property. Ownership of a female was transferred from father to husband. Women had no right to vote, own property, or make a legal contract. Employers and slave owners had the right to physically beat and scourge their employees and slaves in the name of discipline. Males believed they had a divine right to dominate and control women and minorities.

Fortunately, that belief began to change. An awareness of social injustice began to emerge. Laws, along with ongoing social awareness, have made the issue of ownership of human beings unacceptable. Slavery was abolished, women were allowed to vote, and minority citizens gained civil rights.

In 1994, the Violence Against Women Act (VAWA) was passed, which allows government and private organizations to offer assistance to individuals affected by domestic violence.

Domestic violence is a crime, punishable by fine and imprisonment in most states. In recent years, many states have adopted mandatory arrest laws where there is probable cause of domestic assault. The domestic violence law is designed to protect individuals, male and female who are too weak or unskilled to defend themselves from violent attacks. The intent of the law is to stop domestic violence and promote a safe, nonviolent home environment for all family members.

Steps to Stopping Domestic Violence

If you are domestically violent, stay apart from your partner and get professional help. In addition, these are some steps you should take to prevent domestic violence:

Step One: Think neutral thoughts about the use of violence in domestic disputes by asking these questions: "Do I have to use violence in domestic disputes?" "Can I resolve spousal or family conflicts without physical force or violence?" "Is it lawful to use physical force or violence in domestic disputes?"

Step Two: Make three separate lists of the positive, negative, and neutral consequences of using physical force or violence in domestic disputes.

Step Three: Write on an index card all the bad or negative consequences—including police arrest, jail time, and fines, restraining orders from your partner and children, and one-year batterers' treatment program—and carry it with you.

Step Four: Read the negative consequences to yourself as often as possible, especially when you feel tempted to use force or violence in domestic disputes.

Step Five: Associate domestic violence with pain or negative consequences.

Step Six: Associate non-violence with pleasure and positive relationships.

Step Seven: Use meditation or relaxation techniques with deep breathing and positive visualization as methods to prevent domestic violence.

Step Eight: Stay at least two yards distance from relatives, friends, and family members who use physical force or violence towards you.

Step Nine: When you feel stressed, exercise. Go out walking, jogging, bicycling, dancing, swimming, weight lifting, or any other physical activity.

The purpose of the above first five steps is to help you **develop a strong negative belief associated with pain** towards domestic violence. The last four steps are designed to support you in achieving your goal.

Affirmations to Stop Domestic Violence

Say the following to yourself:

- "I do not have to use physical force or violence in my family disputes."
- "The negative outcome of using physical force or violence outweighs the positive outcome."
- "Using physical force or violence is costly and harmful to me and my loved ones."

These affirmations will lead you on your way to de-programming your subconscious beliefs about domestic violence.

Remember that habits have three dimensions. They can be positive, negative, or neutral. You must learn to form positive habits to be successful in life. Learn to balance your habits so that they don't become counterproductive addictions.

Summary

Domestic violence is an issue of controlling by force. The batterer chooses to use force to terrorize his or her date, or partner to display power and authority over them. The term violence is misunderstood by many people, especially by the perpetrators of domestic violence. They tend to identify violence as only murder or homicide, and serious physical assault. However, violence also consists of pushing, shoving, grabbing, slapping, intimidating, name calling, physical or emotional threats, and sex without consent of the other person. Pushing, shoving, grabbing or holding behavior when you and your mate are in a happy mood does not constitute a crime and is not punishable by law. Only when you and/or your partner are angry or does unwanted pushing, shoving, grabbing, or holding become a crime.

Questions

1. What is domestic violence?
2. Why it is not tolerated in our society?
3. How can one stop domestic violence?
4. What are the steps to stop domestic violence?

CONCLUSION

Dear Reader,

We have come to the end of *When Our Leaders Do Bad Things.* Three-dimensional thinking, the modified biological defense mechanisms and the "negative thinking" are simple, powerful tools that, when applied, brings the desired results.

Have you ever felt like hitting or slapping your supporters, customers, boss, co-worker, or partner? Have you ever felt like calling them names? Do you experience anger, frustration, or emotional confusion in your social or personal relationships? Do you feel that talking to your supporters, customers, boss, co-worker, or partner is like talking to a wall? Have there been times you have felt like breaking off your relationships with other people?

If you have understood the tools, principles, and instructions presented in this book, you should now recognize the power that you possess to change your thoughts and transform your feelings and behavior. You have the ability to rebuild your life. You have the power to control not only your greed, lust, and anger, but also other emotions. You can choose to pay attention and enjoy the positive moments and take a "timeout" from the negative moments. With these skills and strategies, you can create happy moments in any situation.

Here are some helpful points to remember:

- Use "three-dimensional thinking" to evaluate problems.
- Choose negotiation, taking a timeout, or freeze (acceptance) to solve problems.
- Think positive thoughts to have physical and mental energy, success, and happiness.
- Think negative thoughts to quit alcohol, drugs, overeating, greed, lust, addictions and counterproductive behavior.
- Think neutral thoughts to reduce and release anger and fear.

Best Regards

Mangal Dan Dipty, Ph.D.

ABOUT THE AUTHOR

Dr. Mangal Dan Dipty lives with his wife, Wendy Dipty, in Las Vegas, Nevada. He was an individual, family, and group psychotherapist in a private practice in Anaheim, California for over fifteen years. His treatment method is eclectic, encompassing Gestalt, cognitive, rational-emotive, and behavioral approaches. He holds a master's degree in social work and a doctorate in clinical psychology.

He has more than twenty-five years of professional experience in his practice as a caseworker, counselor, and administrator. He has been Director of the Riverside County Outpatient Mental Health Clinic and Oral Commissioner of the Board of Behavioral Science Examiners in Southern California. He has provided therapy through a variety of mental health settings including Family Care Centers of Los Angeles and Orange County Emergency Treatment Services.

His workshop and seminar topics include "Decision Making made Easy," "Stress and Anger Management Made Easy," "Styles of Communication for Success," and "Domestic Violence Prevention Strategies" for professionals and general audiences. For more information e-mail at: dr.dipty@mail.com

To give a gift of *When Our Leaders Do Bad Things* to your loved ones or friends, visit Morgan James Publishing or Amazon. com. Meet Dr. Dipty in Las Vegas or online and receive free training or continuing education at www.YourDecisionPlusAction.com.

ABOUT THE BOOK

When Our Leaders Do Bad Things was written to young students and professionals who desire to be our future leaders, priests, and celebrities to bring them more awareness of the significant human weaknesses of ignorance, forgetfulness, and sleepiness. This information aims to help them be aware and constantly prepared so they can avoid mistakes that might cost them their jobs and relationships as well as recognition and prestige. The book also was written to help laypersons that are interested in acquiring wisdom and knowledge about the skills they need to succeed.

There are three psychological power tools presented here:

1. The three-dimensional thinking: a decision-making tool.
2. The biological stress defense mechanism: a tool for taking action immediately

Understanding and applying these first two tools can help individuals choose the best course of action in the midst of emotional confusion, a common plight among leaders and those who live in the limelight.

3. The negative thinking: a precious tool to control passion, addiction, and other emotions such as greed and lust and counterproductive behavior. These tools not only help individuals make the best decisions and take right actions,

they also can help them extinguish anger, frustration, and stress. In addition, this book provides information about styles of communication and ways to enhance one's communication skill.

This book is not designed to treat any psychological disorder or to provide any therapeutic treatment. It was written for healthy, intelligent individuals who desire to increase their knowledge and be successful in every part of their lives.

"Help other people in your chosen field and discover a fortune for yourself"
— Dr. Dipty

BUY A SHARE OF THE FUTURE IN YOUR COMMUNITY

These certificates make great holiday, graduation and birthday gifts that can be personalized with the recipient's name. The cost of one S.H.A.R.E. or one square foot is $54.17. The personalized certificate is suitable for framing and will state the number of shares purchased and the amount of each share, as well as the recipient's name. The home that you participate in "building" will last for many years and will continue to grow in value.

Here is a sample SHARE certificate:

HABITAT FOR HUMANITY

THIS CERTIFIES THAT

YOUR NAME HERE

HAS INVESTED IN A HOME FOR A DESERVING FAMILY

1985-2010

TWENTY-FIVE YEARS OF BUILDING FUTURES
IN OUR COMMUNITY ONE HOME AT A TIME

1200 SQUARE FOOT HOUSE @ $65,000 = $54.17 PER SQUARE FOOT

This certificate represents a tax deductible donation. It has no cash value.

YES, I WOULD LIKE TO HELP!

*I support the work that Habitat for Humanity does and I want to be part of the excitement! As a donor, I will receive periodic updates on your construction activities but, more importantly, I know my gift will help a family in our community realize the dream of homeownership. **I would like to SHARE in your efforts against substandard housing in my community!** (Please print below)*

PLEASE SEND ME _____ SHARES at $54.17 EACH = $ $_____

In Honor Of: _____

Occasion: (Circle One)　　HOLIDAY　　BIRTHDAY　　ANNIVERSARY

　　　OTHER: _____

Address of Recipient: _____

Gift From: _____ *Donor Address:* _____

Donor Email: _____

I AM ENCLOSING A CHECK FOR $ $_____ PAYABLE TO HABITAT FOR HUMANITY <u>OR</u> PLEASE CHARGE MY VISA OR MASTERCARD *(CIRCLE ONE)*

Card Number _____ Expiration Date: _____

Name as it appears on Credit Card _____ Charge Amount $ _____

Signature _____

Billing Address _____

Telephone # Day _____ Eve _____

PLEASE NOTE: Your contribution is tax-deductible to the fullest extent allowed by law.
Habitat for Humanity • P.O. Box 1443 • Newport News, VA 23601 • 757-596-5553
www.HelpHabitatforHumanity.org

9 781614 481447